NEWGRANGE:
THE MYSTERY OF THE CHEQUERED LIGHTS

NEWGRANGE:
THE MYSTERY
OF THE CHEQUERED LIGHTS

Hugh Kearns

NEW
ISLAND

Newgrange: The Mystery of the Chequered Lights
New edition published 2005
by New Island
2 Brookside
Dundrum Road
Dublin 14
www.newisland.ie

First published by Elo Publications, December 1993

ISBN 1 904301 90 8

British Library Cataloguing in Publication Data. A CIP catalogue record for this book is
available from the British Library.

Typeset by New Island
Cover design by New Island
Printed in the UK by Biddles

10 9 8 7 6 5 4 3 2 1

For Sheila

CONTENTS

PREFACE

This book isn't intended to be an 'archaeological' book, but rather a popular, that is, non-professional, re-evaluation of the archaeologists' conclusions. They've done their job, now I'm doing mine, which is to bring an imaginative insight into the subject. By a process of a radical re-examination of the archaeological facts already established, I've arrived at a startling theory that fits not only those facts, but all the antecedent folklore as well.

What follows is a sober, logical analysis of the mechanical structure of Newgrange, a massive Neolithic structure that was built more than 5,000 years ago. According to Professor Michael J. (Brian) O'Kelly of the Department of Archaeology at University College, Cork, who carried out a thorough, professional excavation and restoration of the structure from 1962 to 1975, it was built by a civilisation whose leaders were expert engineers, architects and astronomers. His report, published in 1982, became the foundation stone and bible of reference for me.

The fact that the conclusions arrived at in this book are far-reaching, astonishing, incredible and totally unexpected is no fault of mine, and I claim no responsibility for any upset they may have caused. I take the view that however the facts emerge, they are facts and must be dealt with. Ignoring them won't make them go away.

1

CHEQUERED LIGHTS

The Master Builder of Newgrange worked to an amazingly precise and accurate master plan. That plan is so over- whelmingly spectacular, so breathtakingly vast, that you may have difficulty accepting that a Stone Age culture could even have dreamed of it.

They did more than dream it.

They built their dream in stone. They built it so effectively and so solidly, using the biggest boulders they could find, that it has survived for more than fifty cen- turies. It's so well constructed that it will probably stand for another fifty centuries.

And the master plan still works.

When the archaeological excavators of Newgrange discovered that the massive structure had been cleverly orientated to the winter solstice dawn, most people were totally underwhelmed. It seems everybody knew that already. So a shaft of light shines into the place at midwinter. So what? No one suspected that there was anything more to it than that.

Newgrange became a mildly interesting tourist attraction. Very ancient and all that. Very interesting designs carved into the stones as well. A very old tomb, apparently, with a winter solstice orientation.

But if you run the gauntlet of the narrow passage, squeezing between the two ranks of silent stones, you'll experience a strange feeling, a feeling of being in intimate touch with something mysterious, something unfinished. It will seem to you that the stones are straining to cry out, to tell the whole story.

And the stones do speak.

If you put one stone on top of another, nothing much happens; put two more on top of the first two, and the whole lot will probably fall down sooner or later; put a whole bunch of stones on top of one another, and passers-by will ask you what it's for. It's always for something, otherwise why bother?

Newgrange is no different: the arrangement of the stones still tells the story of what they're for – if you know the language.

There are four practical clues remaining today that reveal the true purpose for which Newgrange was built.[1] They're built into the very stones of the structure itself. They go together in a plain, simple, logical sequence which I am going to reassemble for you. I suspect that when I am finished, you'll come to the same conclusion that I did – that Newgrange is much, much more than just an impressive burial mound, or even a crude early calendar.

I built a scale model of the passage and chamber of Newgrange. Luckily, and only for reasons of convenience, I built it in the old-money scale of 1:24. If I had built it to any other scale, it's very likely that I would have abandoned the whole project in frustration. As it was, it took me nearly two years to get the 1:24 scale version to work.

Actually, that's not strictly true. The model was working fine the whole time, but I just couldn't see it. At that time

I didn't know what I should have been looking for. The Neolithic architect's master plan, even in 1:24 scale, is so vast it wasn't apparent.

Looking back on it now, I'm not surprised.

The model is 1.3 metres in length. I later realised that if I had built it on any smaller of a scale, it would have been too small and too difficult to manipulate in order to orientate it to a light source.

On the other hand, if I had built it on a bigger scale, even the simple physical effort of transporting it would have become a prohibitive burden. Further difficulties would have arisen in attempting to orientate it accurately on the various sites, difficulties that would have strained my limited resources at the time.

As I proceeded with the construction of the 1:24 scale model, the various peculiarities in the structure began to reveal themselves. It began to dawn on me that the Neolithic civil engineers worked with a very high level of precision.

We have been conditioned by modern science to expect 'technology' to possess certain characteristics. We have come to expect scientific and other precision instruments to be squared-off, highly polished and regular, to have sharply defined edges and have neat graduations clearly marked on them. They're also expected to have well-lubricated moving parts and effective calibrating mechanisms. These are the accepted hallmarks of modern 'precision'. We would probably have great difficulty in accepting that any instrument which fails to exhibit these characteristics could work efficiently at all, much less perform with any degree of accuracy or precision. These very desirable characteristics, as I am sure you are well aware, are notably absent from the natural stone structure of Newgrange.

Nevertheless, more and more people are beginning to accept that Newgrange is indeed a highly accurate solar time-measuring device[2] – a two-weeks-to-view calendar page, as I like to describe it.

This has now been fairly well established, not least by Professor Michael J. O'Kelly's pioneering excavation work in the 1960s. Furthermore, it's becoming increasingly apparent that this seemingly crude collection of boulders is actually a remarkable feat of late Stone Age science and precision engineering.

The more research that's carried out on these amazing structures, the more evidence emerges that the popular image of Stone Age people as primitive savages is a serious underestimation of their level of sophistication.

Possibly because they find it hard to accept the truth, many people will still tell you that Newgrange was built by the Celts. The fact is that it was already ancient by the time the first Celtic explorers landed on this island. It had fallen into disuse and was nothing more than a ruin long before the advent of the Celts. It's so ancient that no one today can even remember the name of the people who built it.

But it's also true that a folk memory has survived down to modern times of something special, something extraordinary, linked to this mysterious place.

Strange as it may seem, the secret of what went on at Newgrange is also locked into the legends which were abundantly recorded with the coming of the Christians. There's hardly an early manuscript that doesn't contain some reference to the place, each one stranger than the next.

When I eventually stumbled on the secret in one of the legends, it wasn't exactly like a bolt out of the blue. Quite the opposite, in fact. Because of my work as a graphic designer, I often had occasion to research and investigate Newgrange. The enigmatic, prehistoric graphics carved into the huge stones at this strange place have long been a source of inspiration for artists and graphic designers, myself included. I began to detect a thread of something odd, something common to almost every one of the reference sources.

I found it strange that almost all of the early written references to Newgrange seemed to revolve around the subject of light, such as 'Lords of Light', 'Gods of the Sun',[3] and another quite odd one: 'chequered lights'.

This last reference is found in the book *Colloquy of the Ancients*, a collection of fifteenth- and seventeenth-century manuscripts, which in turn are probably copies of much earlier writings. The words are contained in the reply allegedly given by one of the Tuatha Dé Danann, the supposedly magical race of gods, when asked where he comes from: 'Out of yonder Brú, chequered with the many lights,' he replies. *Brú na Bóinne* – literally, the Mansion of the Boyne – is the ancient name for Newgrange in the Irish language.

All my sources are the various translations into English from the original Irish manuscripts, but I did find the word 'chequered' to be one of those strangely powerful, fundamental words that can leap the chasm of translation between one language and another and still retain an undiluted sense of its meaning.

In the original Irish, the word was *'breatach'* and the root of the word is drawn from the concept of speckled, or spotted, as in the Irish word for trout, *'breac'*, a spotted or speckled fish, giving *'breacadh'*, chequered. In the Irish, daybreak, as in going from dark to light, is *'breacadh an lae'*.

The very concept of 'chequered' in any language, especially when associated with light, generates a powerful image in the mind – images of periodic opposites, of sequences of black and white, of rhythmic patterns of light and dark, of regular repetitions switching on and off between light and dark.

It was this enigmatic and seemingly insignificant phrase, 'chequered with the many lights', that was to be the key piece of the jigsaw for me. It wasn't the complete picture – not by any means – just the important first glimpse of what was to become the amazing Newgrange picture.

It was a beginning, not the end.

It was the start of what turned out to be a five-year search for the answer, an answer which seemed to always be there, just out of reach. Every time I thought I had it in my grasp, it faded away, leaving a tantalising clue, directing me to yet another line of enquiry. It was maddening and frustrating, but I kept chasing it until I finally got hold of it.

In the end, I believe I have found the secret behind the 'chequered lights'. If I am right, then I believe I have also discovered the real, so far unsuspected purpose behind the construction of Newgrange.

I still find it odd that such a powerful phrase as 'chequered lights' should have been allowed to remain in its particular context, in a manuscript of the Christian era. Perhaps it was felt by the authors to be too obscure, too inscrutable, to have been considered a danger.

We all know from our history books that a vital part of the Christianising mission was the eradication of the pagan practices of sun worship. Even St Patrick himself is on record railing against such activity.[4] (It's interesting to note that in *Colloquy of the Ancients*, St Patrick takes time out to confer with his 'guardian angels' as to whether or not talking to pagans would contaminate him, which, of course, they reassure him would not happen; one of his guardian angels is actually called *Solus Breatach*.)

It's only natural, and not entirely unreasonable, for the proprietors of any new religion to discourage the newly converted from relapsing into observance of their previous deities. That frighteningly effective new weapon of the time, the written word, was skilfully employed by the Christian missionaries to attack and undermine the high priests of sun worship, the pagan Druids. That's to say that the Christians focused not on the Celtic Druids, but rather on their predecessors, the Neolithic priests. In fact, the Christians appear to have struck some sort of *entente cordiale* with the Celtic Druids, best expressed in the combination of the two religious symbols of the Christian cross and the Celtic sun wheel in the so-called Celtic cross.

Although the Celtic Druids were the power behind the throne, standing as they did next to the king in status, they were nevertheless extremely vulnerable to the new weapon. They could write, but they considered it a sacrilege to commit their knowledge to writing; everything of their culture was committed to memory.

The Celtic Druids learned all the local folklore as it was told to them by the pre-Celts – the whole repertoire of wonderfully imaginative poetry, song and saga had been passed on orally. In turn, they told and retold what they had learned, enthusiastically carrying on a tradition that was already ancient long before they discovered this island. They never dreamed that when they retold the weird and wonderful stories, they were actually perpetuating a secret, coded dictionary of the people's knowledge.

Because the people didn't tell them the whole story.

As we shall see, it's quite clear that the people only parted with enough of their knowledge to keep their new Celtic overlords happy.

There's an ancient Irish, probably pre-Celtic, *sean-fhocal*, or proverb, which goes: 'I won't tell you everything I know, because you would then be wiser than I am myself.' It's like an Irish code of silence, an Irish version of the Sicilian *omerta*, if you like. It's not a code of total silence, though – it wouldn't be Irish if it were – but more of an Irish 'need-to-know' code: I'll only tell you as much as *you* think you need to know. Do not volunteer information. Keep the onus on the enquirer.

Later on, the Christian missionaries, who, like all scribes, wrote with a clear strategy in mind, suffered a similar fate. It's the writer's choice as to how much of the original will remain in a retold local saga and in what manner the story will be edited, embellished or amended for propaganda purposes, but before anyone can rewrite any well-known story, they must be fully conversant with the complete and unabridged original.

The pen is mightier than the sword, but only when it's sharpened on the whetstone of fact.

Fortunately – or unfortunately, depending on your point of view – the people also left the Christians a couple of bricks short of a load.

Just like the Celtic Druids before them, the people hadn't given them the full story, therefore they couldn't tell with certainty which were the important bits of the early sagas, which is probably the reason why they left that powerful phrase, 'chequered with the many lights', in place in the new manuscripts.

They didn't know how important it was because nobody told them.

They were neither the first nor the last victims of that ancient Irish *sean-fhocal*, or proverb: 'I won't tell you everything I know, because you would then be wiser than I am myself.'

2

ORIGINS

A remarkably green and fertile little island, Ireland is a strange place, blessed with a kindly climate of soft winter mists and summer rain. Such mildness belies the northerly position of the island, in latitudes where it would be reasonable to expect it to be cooler.

This uncommonly temperate habitat has to do with the Gulf Stream, a current of water that bathes the island in its warmth, carried all the way from the Gulf of Mexico on the other side of the Atlantic.

As well as that, the island is the first land to meet the prevailing westerly winds, heavily pregnant with the moist Atlantic air. The risk of drought isn't something the various new arrivals ever had to worry about. Throughout its 80,000 square kilometres you'll discover countless lakes and an abundance of rivers, great and small, where salmon and trout abound. In some parts of the island, it can seem there isn't a hill that doesn't have a lake at the foot of it.

We can stand on the west coast of Ireland today and look out across the wild salt ocean toward the sunset, knowing that there's no more land between us and the New World 3,000 uneasy, windswept miles away, too far for the early migrants in prehistory to have attempted a crossing. No doubt some tried, never to be heard of again. If some of the taller tales of pre-Columbus exploration are to be believed, one or two may even have made it, who knows? But for the rest of their compatriots, this was it. The last stop.

They were all, in their time, eventually cast up on this island terminus, the last piece of dry land on the north-western edge of the continent, and looking at the new Europe, it seems that nothing has really changed.

These waves of migratory and other influences are more evident today, since Ireland became a member of the European Community. Some of these influences are more visible than others. For instance, the landscape painter's palette has been radically changed. The once proverbial forty shades of green have recently been augmented with the introduction of the startlingly bright, yellow-green fields of rape. Rapeseed is now a valuable crop, prized for its oil content, allegedly destined to break the Middle East fuel cartels.

As you travel about, you'll also notice the dark green patches spreading on the upland slopes – the vigorous, softwood proclamation of a renewal of our once-great hardwood forests. The revival of forestry is just one more of the alternative agricultural activities being encouraged by the new Europe. (The fact that the aerosols exhaled by the evergreen fir trees causes the uplands to be wreathed in a perennial blue haze seems not to bother the beurocrats in the slightest, nor does the fact that the pine forests are sterile, supporting little or no wildlife, or that they acidify the watercourses to the detriment of the fish life.)

Soaring above all these scenic experiments, safe (for the moment) from interference are the spectacular mountain vistas, especially on the rugged west coast, where the ever-changing light paints and repaints the landscape in a different mood from day to day, sometimes hour to hour.

On the tops of many of the mountains stand great stone constructions. They're the dormant remnants of a long-forgotten civilisation, a culture so ancient that they have no name to be remembered by. Not even the Europeans remember anything about them. There are those[1] who say they may not have come from Europe at all, that they came instead from the west.

Wherever they came from, they certainly knew how to build impressive stone buildings. These enigmatic structures, constructed with huge boulders, or megaliths (the generic archaeological term for them), often contain internal stone-roofed passages and chambers. Typically occupying prominent sites, they invariably hold commanding views of the surrounding countryside.

The generic name Shee, or in Irish, *Sídhe*, meaning spirit or fairy, has traditionally been applied to these structures and to the prominences on which they stand. Examples include *Cnocsídhe*, the Hill or Mount of the Fairies, and *Sídhe Mór*, the Big Fairy Mound, usually so named to distinguish it from other, similar but lesser features present in the same locality; these smaller ones will most likely be called *Sídhe Beag*, the Little Fairy Mound.

There are many other stone structures of a completely different type at lower levels, which have been known, and in fact are still known, by such fanciful names as fairy forts, giant's beds and Druid's altars.

On the opposite side of the island, about halfway along the east coast, where the land becomes flatter and less scenic, is the mouth of the Boyne, an otherwise unexceptional salmon and trout river.

The east coast runs virtually on a line north-south, and the Boyne River, for all intents and purposes, flows west to east. In common with other east coast salmon rivers, the Boyne is what's known as an 'early' river: there's a run of spawning salmon in winter. In modern times, the official salmon angling season on the Boyne opens on the first day of February.

Less than half a day's stroll upstream on the northern bank of the Boyne, just beyond the limit of the tidal effect, is a small, grassy hill. It's a perfectly ordinary hill, just another in a series of unremarkable small hills which form part of a low ridge. Rising to barely 60 metres at a distance of one kilometre from the river, this ridge forms the northern rim of the Boyne Valley.

In an island so well endowed with spectacular and desirable sites, this little hill doesn't appear to have much to recommend it to the discerning developer. Even the view from the top isn't in any way inspiring.

To the north the land becomes less fertile and more broken, rising to nearly 200 metres around the village of Collon, 10 kilometres away. There's nothing to excite the eye unless the weather permits sight of the Cooley Mountains, sometimes visible in the far distance.

Facing south-eastwards, the land immediately slopes gently down to the valley floor 60 metres below, where the Boyne River meanders through the floodplain about one kilometre away. On the far bank, it immediately rises steeply, forming the slightly higher horizon on the far side of the valley.

But it was here, on this unremarkable hill in this uninspiring setting, that a Master Builder of that forgotten Stone Age society decided for some peculiar reason to erect a unique and controversial stone-roofed building. Not just another one of the same type as before – no, it was to be a special, spectacular, one-of-a-kind building that would outshine all previous ones, and which was destined to become enshrined in folklore and legend forever.

That stone building, now known as Newgrange, has survived, perched on its little hill, for more than 5,000 years. It's older by 800 years than the pyramids of Egypt and it's much older than Stonehenge in England. This latter reference is perhaps an unfair comparison, because Stonehenge doesn't actually qualify as a 'building' – it doesn't ever seem to have been roofed, whereas the pyramids do contain a number of roofed chambers and passages within them.

It's generally accepted that the pyramids were built for just one purpose: as splendid tombs for the Egyptian pharaohs, who were ceremoniously laid to rest accompanied by their self-sacrificing servants, along with fortunes in precious ornaments of gold, the sun metal. The purpose for which Newgrange was built was not as immediately clear, and the consequent debate as to whether or not it, too, was designed as a royal tomb continues to this day.

The pyramids were sealed by Egyptian stonemasons after the funeral ceremonies with all manner of ingenious but mostly unsuccessful false entrances and blind passages, designed to frustrate the efforts of grave robbers who coveted the golden treasures.

Newgrange, too, was sealed after its completion, the difference in this case being that the process was accidental. The outer mantle collapsed in prehistory, burying the entrance and preserving the interior passage and chamber fully intact down to recent times.

Whether or not this collapse was precipitated by a hostile act of man or, as seems far more likely, by natural causes such as an earth tremor,[2] no attempt appears to have been made to restore the structure in ancient times. It had survived in this state of collapse, with the vital clues to its special purpose fortuitously sealed from interference and destruction.

Meanwhile, all knowledge of its builders gradually faded into extinction in the memory of the people. By the time the Celts began arriving on the island, Newgrange was already ancient.

Strangely, the knowledge of the existence of something special at this place lived on in the folklore of the pre-

Celtic people, and that folklore survived intact until the coming of the Christians, bringing with them the fantastic new technology of the written word.

There's hardly an early Christian manuscript that doesn't contain some reference to Newgrange. It's usually described as the dwelling place of gods, kings or, in one instance, as the abode of 'three times fifty sons of kings'.[3]

In many of the early written references,[4] the Boyne River is closely associated with the building, sometimes as a marital union of god and goddess. The Boyne was a goddess, and the Good God, Daghda, lived in Newgrange with his son Aengus. Newgrange is sometimes referred to as *Brúgh Aenghus,* the House or Palace of Aengus.

The Boyne River itself is often at the centre of legends concerning the dissemination of knowledge. The Salmon of Knowledge was caught from the waters of the Boyne and cooked over an open fire by Fionn MacCumhail, a legendary hero of the Tuatha Dé Danann. Fionn apparently burned his thumb, allegedly attempting to stop a blister from forming on the skin of the roasting fish. Instinctively putting his thumb in his mouth to cool it, Fionn found that he had knowledge of all things. Any time he wished to know anything thereafter, he simply sucked his thumb.

Many Irish people think that Newgrange was built by the Celts. They know full well that the Celts have only been here for the proverbial Irish 'wet day' – meaning for a very short time – but the Celtic fiction is proffered in order to keep the tourists happy. If a visitor were to query the truth of it, they would likely get another pure Celtic response: 'Ah, sure, what harm, it's so long ago another couple of thousand years will make no difference.' All timeframes are elasticated in Ireland, historic as well as modern. It has been said that there are approximately a dozen words in the Irish language equivalent to the Spanish *manāna,* none of which manage to convey the same sense of urgency.

What's now known for certain, though, is that Newgrange was in the course of construction in or around 3,200 BC and that its outer covering slipped, tumbled or otherwise fell down at some point after that, probably still in the prehistoric period.

With the benefit of hindsight, we can say that the catastrophe of Newgrange's collapse was most fortunate because, paradoxically, it succeeded where the later pyramid builders failed: in protecting the building from being plundered, perhaps even destroyed, at the hands of the various immigrants who were to arrive here in the course of the succeeding millennia. It's only because of this fortunate accident that Newgrange, that unique and controversial example of earliest stone architecture, survived intact until 1699 AD, when it was rediscovered.

What isn't known exactly, even now, is when that catastrophic collapse occurred, but it was certainly long enough after its completion for the structure to have become famous. It must have been prior to the arrival of the Celts because they knew nothing of the true nature of the structure.

Even though the collapse had occurred before the arrival of the Celts, their Druids readily adopted Newgrange into their pantheon of sacred places. Yet they could only have come to know of its importance from the oral tradition of the natives. Isn't it strange, though, that they don't appear to have known of the existence of the passage and chamber within the collapsed mound?

Professor O'Kelly's investigation clearly showed that they had both remained undisturbed until modern times.[5] Furthermore, not one of the surrounding richly carved kerbstones had been unearthed until after the rediscovery of the entrance.

Had the Celts discovered the entrance, or even the surrounding kerbstones, the incised designs left by the previous, unknown culture would presumably have influenced Celtic design; they would have been just as impressed as we are with the prehistoric art. Given their tendency to adopt local rites, rituals and customs, it isn't unreasonable to suppose that they would have melded the spirals, lozenges, chevrons and other graphic forms from the stones at Newgrange into their own artistic expression.

But in all that time, the remembrance of something special about this place, Newgrange, remained in the oral tradition of the people, handed down from generation to generation, woven into complex and fantastic stories, even though it was never fully explained or even spoken of plainly.[6] Which is another good example of the power of that old Irish proverb: 'I won't tell you everything I know, because you would then be wiser than I am myself.'

3

REDISCOVERY

Ironically, the rediscovery of Newgrange happened quite by accident. The landowner, a man named Campbell, had his labourers begin to excavate what he thought was a windfall deposit of perfect road-building stones, a sort of 'instant quarry', all neatly piled together under a grassy mound on top of a hill on his newly acquired farm.

No self-respecting Irishman would ever have willingly risked digging into a 'fairy mound', as such features in the Irish landscape are known, in fear of the retribution of the 'little people', or fairies, who live in them. Pagan though its origins may be, the tradition can still be seen on many family farms around the country in the pattern of ploughing, where the tractor so often carefully avoids these mysterious mounds, remnants of a prehistory that have stubbornly refused to be obliterated.

In fact, Newgrange itself stands in the middle of a working farm, and if you look south-east from the monument down into the river valley, about one kilometre away, you can pick out at least two such mounds which have not yet been excavated. They stand in the crop fields, the larger one fenced off to prevent grazing livestock from trampling and eroding it; this one is known as Site B. Slightly nearer and a little to the west of Site B stands Site A, the smaller of the two, which is surrounded by a low bank, the outline of which grows fainter with the years, yet the mound itself continues to stand, defiant.

It seems reasonable, then, to surmise that Mr Campbell's labourers were probably immigrants, imported by the new landowner to do the job. Mr Campbell himself would appear to have been a Williamite 'planter', the pejorative term for those who had been granted confiscated land for loyal services to King William of Orange.

Incidentally, the famous Battle of the Boyne, which is still going on, was fought just downstream of Newgrange, hardly a cannon shot away, on 12 July 1690 when King William III of Orange, a Dutch Protestant, aided by a regiment of Prussian Huzzars donated by the Pope, wrested the English throne from the Scottish, Catholic King James II and his Catholic French allies.

It was only nine short years later that Mr Campbell set about his quarrying, which is hardly enough time for him to have established trusting relationships with the local, Catholic workforce – hence the outsourced labourers.

As Professor O'Kelly's late colleague and wife, Claire, remarked, 'Would he have dared otherwise to plunder the House of Aonghus of the Brugh? The native population were no doubt well acquainted with the traditions associated with the mound...but did not share their knowledge with their alien landlords.'[1] (There's that ancient proverb again: 'I won't tell you everything I know...'.)

You can imagine the excitement that followed on all sides in that winter of 1699, when the worst fears of the locals were dramatically confirmed by the sudden appearance of an unnatural structure, complete with strange carvings on the walls and ceiling, unlike anything ever seen before, buried under the fairy mound.

The Anglo-Irish Establishment of the time could not accept that the mere peasant Irish could ever have been capable of building such an imposing edifice, so they attributed it instead to the Viking raiders of the ninth and tenth centuries, building tombs for their leaders killed in battles here. Newgrange and other structures like it came to be known as 'Danish mounts and forts'.

Had the latest landlord taken any heed of the structure's original name in the Irish language, for instance, or had he shown any respect for the rich folklore associated with this ancient place, he might have left himself open to the risk of discovering the true origins of Newgrange.[2]

In contrast, Charles Vallancey, a British army surveyor variously credited with the rank of major, colonel and even general, took a great shine to Ireland and all things Irish when he arrived here in 1750 to conduct a survey of natural resources. He even studied the language, and on occasion was inclined to produce his signature in an Irish form as *Cathal Ua Bhallansaí*. It was Vallancey who first proposed an astronomical purpose for Newgrange, a theory which was dismissed as nonsense at the time.[3]

Like any other victorious invader, the English naturally considered that their language should be imposed on the vanquished incumbents, just as the invading Irish Celts had done to the English some ten centuries before.[4] One of the great tragedies resulting from this policy was the wholesale effacement of the beautifully descriptive Irish place names throughout the island. A hodgepodge of similar-sounding, but spurious, English words was substituted. Mercifully, there's at least a consistency within this system of phonetic alternatives; in most cases, the derivation can still be recovered, teased out of the mock anglification. It's difficult to say how much of our knowledge of the past has been lost due to this imposed system of phonetic substitution.

As the database of knowledge expanded on the Newgrange-type structures, the late Victorian and early twentieth-century archaeologists revised their origins further and further back in time. George Coffey, for instance, predicted a Neolithic origin for Newgrange itself as early as 1912.[5]

Based on the system originated by Christian Thomsen (1788–1865), the curator of the National Museum of Denmark, and mindful of the dangers of misinterpretation which would surely arise if they used plain language, the archaeologists opted instead for one or other, and sometimes both, of the Classic languages of Greek and Latin. Both of these older, more stable languages were basic constituents of education in the Western world at that time.

Soon, the late Stone Age structures were being classified as 'Neolithic megalithic tumuli'. In this instance *neo* = new, *mega* = big and *lithos* = stone, all derived from the Greek; and *tumulus*, which comes from the Latin, means tomb. A loose rendering of the original phrase would therefore be 'the new Stone Age big stone tombs'.

The nineteenth-century antiquarians believed that their classically derived nomenclature would serve as a universally understood system of classification. And so it did, enabling communication on the subject between scholars of different nationalities. (Naturally, the knowledge could only be shared among those fortunate enough to have been schooled in the Classics.)

These days, plain and simple English would appear to be a much more pragmatic means of exchange for all these things. After all, modern English is perfectly suited to other, highly technical situations which are shared across nationalities, such as air traffic control and shipping.

But what appears to be an increase in the use of plain English by modern antiquarians isn't exactly what it seems. Ironically, it's generally the case that the modern English technical vocabulary actually has its roots in Latin and Greek. Modern English, a living language, has absorbed the Classical influences into everyday usage.

Like most other anglicised Irish place names, the name 'Boyne' is merely a mock-English phonetic bastardisation which fractures the link to the traditions associated with the original name of the river. In the Irish, or Gaelic, language, the original name is *an Bóinn*, derived from the Gaelic word for cow, which is *Bó*. In Irish mythology, the female water deity, *Boann*, is often represented as a cow. In the case of the Boyne, the river itself was the goddess, and she was allegedly married to the Good God, Dagda, who lived, incredibly, in Newgrange, along with his son Aengus. Of course, it wasn't called Newgrange then, but *Brúgh na Bóinne*, which translates as 'the Mansion of the Boyne'. The English name, Newgrange, is much more recent. It arises from the fact that the surrounding land was an out-farm, or grange, belonging to the Cistercian monks of nearby Mellifont Abbey.

Since the time of its rediscovery in 1699, various official and unofficial bodies have made many efforts to investigate, analyse and otherwise understand the purpose behind the structure of Newgrange. Since that time, also, generations of Irish, English and international scholars and archaeologists, both amateur and professional, have contributed great volumes of speculative writings on the supposed origins and purposes of the structure.

Some of these writings have unwittingly caused more confusion than enlightenment, and sometimes not a little dismay. It's from these scholarly tomes that we learn that over the years there have been a number of crude attempts at excavating the structure – thankfully with little success.

For example, take the unblushing report[6] dating from the 1870s from the pen of an otherwise sensible-sounding gentleman, describing his bungling attempts at so-called excavation. In horrific detail he tells us how he tried to unearth, by brute force, what later transpired to be the lintel of the all-important 'roof-box', later to be uncovered in a properly conducted excavation. He proudly informs us that although he employed two men with crowbars to attempt this 'excavation', he desisted before any real damage was done. Had he persevered in this assault and succeeded in either dislodging or breaking the lintel, one thing is certain: the key to a number of the functions of Newgrange would have been lost forever.

A by-product of the Industrial Revolution in England was the idle sons of the newly rich. Many of these nineteenth-century gentlemen of leisure took up antiquarian pursuits as a sort of fashionable hobby. It became all the rage to slope off to the colonies, dig up a piece of the local heritage and cart it off home to England for display as some sort of archaeological trophy.

Ireland didn't escape these attentions, but, happily, the very size of the megalithic structures ensured their survival. They were fortunately too massive and too well put together, and all except for some small but important pieces, now missing, which were recorded as extant in the newly rediscovered Newgrange, survive. These amateur archaeologists mostly contented themselves instead with the pursuit of smaller game, such as the *Sheela-na-gigs*.

These stone-carved fertility symbols were to be found in abundance, adorning ruined abbeys and early Christian churches around the country. Some of the female representations were crudely explicit and became a favourite target for the heritage hunters. Unknown quantities of them are alleged to have disappeared in the nineteenth century, and very few examples remain.

In passing, there's one in particular which was still in use for fertility rituals as late as the 1970s. It's still to be found, high up in the wall, above one of the tall, narrow windows of a ruined abbey in a west Cork cemetery. All over Ireland, there are traditional, local rituals honouring various Christian saints of antiquity. These annual rites usually take the form of circumambulations, where the pilgrims follow a circular path, stopping at recognised 'stations' to recite prayers. Similarly, in this west Cork cemetery there was a well-beaten path through the lush meadow, starting from under the window, circling back around the ruined abbey, to the inside of the same window. The masonry of the windowsill had been worn smooth by the feet of the pilgrims, who apparently squeeze themselves out through the narrow window in a symbolic representation of birth. Various trinkets, posies of wild flowers and other offerings were placed in niches beside the window.

As for the megalithic structures in the nineteenth century, theories about them abounded. And there were some wild theories! While most early writers attributed the building of Newgrange to the Danes, according to the archaeologist Professor Michael J. O'Kelly, 'influences were also invoked from Egypt, India, Ethiopia, Phœnicia, Celtic Gaul, and so on; in fact, almost any nation under the sun was considered eligible save for the natives themselves.'[7]

Between one theory and another, however, it became the nineteenth-century academic consensus[8] that a late Bronze Age funerary origin for the building would be henceforth deemed appropriate. Irish authorities of the time developed the more-or-less officially held view that its origins were probably Bronze Age, but perhaps somewhat earlier. According to Professor O'Kelly, Newgrange was officially 'regarded as a Bronze Age monument of perhaps 1500 BC or later.'[9]

And so things remained until a comprehensive excavation and restoration of Newgrange was finally undertaken by Professor O'Kelly. The work was carried out seasonally from 1962 to 1975 at the behest of Bórd Fáilte Éireann (the Irish state tourist board, now Fáilte Ireland), who funded the initial works.

Professor O'Kelly set out on this archaeological odyssey, which was to occupy him and his team for almost two decades, with very little precedent on which to base any expectations. It was not the first Neolithic structure to be investigated in Ireland, but it was to be the first occasion on which such a comprehensive excavation and restoration of such a large Neolithic structure was to be undertaken. There had been many such privately sponsored excavations carried out in England, mostly in the nineteenth century, many of which can now be classified, with the benefit of hindsight, as having been nothing more than treasure-hunting vandalism.[10]

During this excavation, however, Professor O'Kelly was to painstakingly dismantle most of the structure and rebuild it, straightening the stones lining the interior passage in the process. He went even further, relieving the interior passage of the weight of its overburden with a cleverly hidden concrete structure. Access to the inside of this structure was to be provided so that investigators of the future could view the hidden sides of the passage stones.

Every small step of the way was carefully recorded and catalogued, culminating in his comprehensive and scholarly report,[11] published in 1982. It's this report that, naturally, became the 'bible' of reference for my own investigations.

One of the most important and exciting facts uncovered by Professor O'Kelly was the true measure of the structure's age. Carbon dating techniques applied to samples of burned earth used in the original construction and corrected by dendrochronology,[12] a modern dating technique using a continually updated database of tree rings that have been calibrated to cover the period, shows that the construction of Newgrange was in progress around 3200 BC, which made it much, much older than the previous best estimates.

These vital findings put a stop to any speculation on the matter of the structure's age. There was to be no more educated guess work – for the first time, it had finally been established, by means of the most modern, nuclear technology, that the building was 52 centuries old. To put it in context, that's 32 centuries before the birth of Christ;

five centuries before the first pyramid was begun in Egypt; 10 centuries before Stonehenge was re-erected in England and an impressive 24 centuries before the first Celts are generally supposed to have arrived in Ireland.

The building is in fact so ancient that neither the Vikings nor the Celts could any longer be held responsible for its existence. It could no longer be thought of as Bronze Age, either, but rather as a Neolithic, or late Stone Age, structure.

Professor O'Kelly made one other particularly startling discovery. Much to his astonishment, he found that the structure is deliberately orientated so that a shaft of light from the midwinter sunrise enters through what he called the 'roof-box', an aperture above the main entrance. This phenomenon was observed by Professor O'Kelly himself[13] at dawn on 21 December 1969 as the shaft of sunlight penetrated the full length of the narrow passage to the central chamber, a distance of 25 metres. The astonishing astronomical skill and precision of the forgotten Stone Age society was being demonstrated once again, performing exactly as they had designed it 52 centuries earlier.

That was neither the first nor the last time that Professor O'Kelly was to be surprised by this strange building. His thorough report is punctuated with his expressions of wonderment at the skill, precision and planning ability of the 'Master Builder' of Newgrange, as he dubbed the anonymous architect. Over a period of nearly two decades, Professor O'Kelly was to come to the realisation that what had been built here, on this strange site, was far removed from 'the simply-constructed rounded mound of water-rolled pebbles that superficial examination had suggested.'[14]

4

TODAY

Today, Newgrange stands restored in all its white quartz-covered glory, almost as it was in the beginning.[1] The double rank of standing stones forming the interior passage have been straightened up, and the only apparent difference between the past and present is in the arrangement of the entrance area.

In the restoration, the entrance was rearranged slightly to facilitate the increased number of visitors expected. At last count,[2] 120,000 people have been coming annually to see this amazing structure, unique among all the world's early stone-roofed buildings. In 1993, Newgrange was declared a World Heritage Site by UNESCO; this coveted status, one of only two in Ireland, the other being Skellig Michael, places Newgrange in the exalted company of the Grand Canyon, the pyramids in Egypt, the Great Wall of China, the Acropolis, the Kremlin, Troy, the Temples of Malta and, of course, Stonehenge.

Newgrange has been in state care since 1882, first under the provisions of the English administration's Protection of Ancient Monuments Act; the responsible body was the-then Board of Public Works. Their successors under Irish legislation, the National Monuments Act 1930, was the Board of Works, latterly the Office of Public Works (OPW), who carry on an unbroken tradition of applying the highest quality of workmanship in the care and restoration of Ireland's historic buildings. It was the National Parks and Monuments Branch of the OPW which carried out the actual restoration work at Newgrange[3] in collaboration with Professor O'Kelly.

There have been major developments at Newgrange in recent times, including the opening of the Brú na Bóinne Visitor Centre downstream, on the south side of the river, in 1997. Direct access to the monuments is no longer allowed, so visitors must proceed through the interpretive centre to a shuttle bus terminal, from where parties of 30 or so visitors at a time are bussed to the monuments of Knowth (a similar passage tomb) and Newgrange. Visitors are then taken in groups up the slope, to stand outside the entrance. Because of the nature of the building, with only one entrance, they must wait here until the party already inside emerges.

While waiting, the visitors are given a short lecture, during which the guides tend to concentrate on the burial theme, thus perpetuating the idea that Newgrange is primarily a tomb. Admittedly, the lecture then usually ends with the declaration that no one really knows who built it, or why it was built.

As well as the standard tour, a much smaller group of people crams into the chamber before dawn on the twenty-first of December every year, the morning of the winter solstice (the word 'solstice' is derived from the Greek, and means 'sun's standstill'). To be precise, it's the dawn after the longest night of the year, when the sun appears to stand in the same place as the previous dawn, and not, as is generally supposed, the dawn of the shortest day.

This smaller group is composed of the privileged few who won admission to the chamber by lottery (application forms are available at the reception desk in the visitor centre; in 2003 nearly 20,000 applications were submitted). They are there in the hope of witnessing the phenomenon of the real light of the real solstice dawn penetrating all the way to the back of the chamber into which they have all crowded.

And every year the same mistake is made: they fail to close up the front entrance, so the spill of sunlight into the open passageway weakens the effect of the beam entering through the roof-box, and little enough of that light gets through, due to the fact that some of the stones lining the passage still lean inwards, cutting off an appreciable amount of the beam.

We will see later on that the roof-box admits the rays of the sun for about a week[4] on either side of the solstice. This discovery has given rise to the false impression that Newgrange was therefore not very accurately aligned.

The popular notion is that the structure was designed so that the sun only enters on the one morning, that of the solstice. That's not actually the case: it's deliberately designed so that about 14 dawns enter.

It has also recently been discovered that the orientation of the structure is in fact designed to admit the rays of the full moonrise once every four and a half years. On the last occasion, in July 2003, the sky was clouded over so there was no show. This particular moonrise appears at a point on the horizon which is further south than the winter solstice sunrise, and does not appear to have been mentioned in any of the legends or early manuscripts.

5

THE PRE-CELTS

Newgrange isn't the oldest surviving stone-roofed building in the world, but it's certainly unique in all the world. Yet the authors of practically every history book appear to be blissfully unaware of that fact.

Most histories give no more than a passing nod in the direction of Newgrange, writing it off, just as Professor O'Kelly did in the beginning, as a crude mound of rubble. Its only saving grace was that this particular mound of rubble appeared to be somewhat ancient, so ancient that there wasn't really any hard factual knowledge about it. Certainly not enough facts to divert scholars bent on the pleasure of sifting through the gold, bronze and iron treasures of slightly later times.

Generally speaking, all you find in most history books is the regulation couple of quick pages on the Fomorians, the Firbolgs, the Tuatha Dé Danann and then on to Celtic history. To be fair, there isn't much romance or excitement in heaps of old rubble. Neither is it fair to expect disciplined historians to become involved in speculation about a time which is more properly referred to as prehistory.

One of the unfortunate consequences of this lamentable failure to apply the historian's discipline to the subject is that any comment that might happen to be made in all innocence by archaeologists tends not to be closely examined, and by default becomes written in stone, so to speak. If that innocent speculation is repeated often enough, it becomes holy writ.

For example, although archaeologists always refer to Newgrange as a 'passage tomb', that description was never intended to mean that it was used *exclusively* for burials. In fact, it's widely accepted by scholars that it was constructed for use in other ceremonial and religious rites, as well as for calendar and funeral purposes. It's important to understand that these pre-Celtic people also used their buildings as calendars – massive calendars, granted, but fairly accurate calendars all the same. (Perhaps they should be more properly referred to as observatories, since a calendar is an abstract, artificial regulator of time.)

Professor George Eogan, who has been investigating Newgrange's sister structure of Knowth since 1962, has this to say on the subject: 'It may well be that the remains were kept until a special day on which they were committed to the tomb. If this was the case, one could assume that other ceremonies were part of the burial rite, some perhaps taking place in the open air.'[1]

Unfortunately, it remains the popular impression that Newgrange is officially regarded merely – and only – as a burial place. That's the equivalent of claiming that the cathedrals of Christchurch, Westminster, Notre Dame and Köln were built as tombs just because the remains of some notable people can be found in them.

One final, important piece of information remains to be announced as a result of Professor O'Kelly's work: the radiocarbon dating of burned human remains, which O'Kelly discovered buried in the floor of the chamber, have not yet been published.[2] It may well be that they weren't completed in time for inclusion in his report in 1982. However, if it is the case that the remains found in Newgrange have proved *not* to be ancient, then obviously they cannot have been placed there by the builders of Newgrange; they must have been deposited there in more modern times.

On the other hand, if they have been found to be just as ancient as the building itself, then it would be conclusive evidence that the design of Newgrange did indeed include a funerary purpose. When it is finally and conclusively shown to have been designed as a tomb, as undoubtedly it will, there still remains yet one more purpose, so far unsuspected, for which the building was erected.

Factual, physical and undeniable evidence that fully explains this other function is contained in a number of structural peculiarities in the building itself. There's much other supporting evidence as well in the landscape adjacent to the site. All of this evidence has survived because it's locked into the very structure of the building and the surrounding terrain. There are also more abstract clues to this other function, contained in legend and folklore.

Although the answer to the Newgrange enigma is blindingly simple once you've seen it, it nevertheless takes some time to put the sequence of clues into a coherent order. When we have examined their methods and understand something of what their intentions were, we will then go back in time to the small grassy hill on the ridge above the Boyne and observe the building of Newgrange from the ground up.

Most early manuscripts contain at least some reference to Newgrange, with the Boyne River usually associated with it. The surviving written references are from the twelfth century and later, copied from manuscripts first produced in early Christian times, from the fifth century AD onwards. They were written in either Irish or Latin, since the English language hadn't yet been developed. Newgrange would have been 36 centuries old at the time.

There are many written references linking Newgrange with the Boyne River, which flows by it. These associations are usually in various 'unions' of the gods. The Boyne was female, Newgrange was male, and they were married, so the legends say.[3]

Local folklore which has persisted down to modern times claims that one particular sunrise entered the chamber at Newgrange. It was Professor O'Kelly's discovery of the famous 'roof-box', as he described it at the time, that led to the confirmation of the local folklore. The roof-box is a narrow horizontal slit situated above the entrance to the building, through which the rays of the midwinter sunrise enter the interior chamber shortly after dawn. The fact that the passage from the entrance is only one metre wide and the total distance from the roof-box to the back of the chamber is 25 metres will give you some idea of the incredible accuracy of the construction.

According to Professor O'Kelly, it's clear that the builders of Newgrange worked to a very precise plan and worked from extremely accurate observations.[4] It would also seem that they erected something unique. Of the thousands of surviving Neolithic structures to be found in Britain and the European mainland, not one of them possesses any equivalent of the roof-box feature. None of these other structures seem to have attracted the attention of the early writers, either.

One would have expected that the inevitable and immediate consequence of finally and conclusively settling the question of who *didn't* build Newgrange would have been renewed interest in discovering who *did* build it. Yet the answer remains as before – no one knows.

Some progress has been made, however. Based on other work on the subject, Professor O'Kelly has now established fairly satisfactorily that the builders of Newgrange were wealthy farmers.[5] They would appear to have been well settled and making a more than comfortable living by farming the rich land in the vicinity; the Boyne Valley still contains some of the richest farmland on the island.

Only such a wealthy culture could possibly have produced the engineers, architects and artisans capable of erecting such a well put together and long-lasting building.

They must also have been a highly motivated and politically well-led society to have been capable of organising the colossal amount of labour required to gather, transport and erect the hundreds of thousands of tonnes of material required for the task.

The pre-Celts display one other important trait to which, again, none of the modern historians seem to have paid much attention: they were obviously a peace-loving people.

The huge number of defensive earthworks, banks and ditches and all the ruined walled enclosures that have so far been catalogued from all over Ireland all belong to a much later time. Even at Newgrange, the premier Neolithic site, nothing of a defensive nature ever seems to have been built. Even wooden stakes driven into the ground to form palisades would have left some evidence of their existence. Nothing of that nature has yet been found. Besides which, it would be surprising if a people who were so adept at building with stone had used anything other than stone for their defences. And no defences means no attackers.

What sort of people were they, then, who could afford to build such magnificent megalithic structures all over the landscape, with no defences around them? What of the hunter-gatherers who followed the herds, living off the land, plundering all before them? Or how were all the building workers' families protected from wild animals? They must have been very vulnerable working in the fields producing the great quantities of food that must have been required to feed the army of builders. How did they defend the builders while at the same time protecting the artisans, those who stayed at home to make clothes and implements and all the other things that the builders would have needed every day?

What did they use for weapons? Were any weapons found? Archaeologists always find lots of beads when they dig out these Neolithic places – war-like stuff, indeed.

So who were they? No one yet knows.

However, the original and, for me, much more intriguing questions still remained unanswered by all these revelations about Newgrange. What were the chequered lights? What was the purpose behind them? How were they chequered?

It was becoming clear to me that I was dealing with yet another example of that Irish *sean-fhocal*: 'I won't tell you everything I know, because you would then be wiser than I am myself.'

6

'WHAT IS THE STARS?'

It will help greatly in the telling of this story if I give the people who built Newgrange a name, one that acknowledges their mastery of the knowledge of the sun's movements, so I propose Na Solasídhe.

'Na Solasídhe' would translate directly from the Irish as 'the Spirits of Light'. *Solas*, pronounced 'sullus', is the Irish for 'light'; it also happens to echo the word '*sol*', the word for 'sun' in other languages. *Sídhe*, pronounced 'shee', is an old Irish word for spirit, or fairy. There were many types of *sídhe* ('shee'), including the dreaded banshee, who was believed to be heard keening, or wailing, by the family of the soon-to-be-dead. 'Shee' is also the word that was used generically to name practically all the prehistoric mounds. One that most often appears is Sheemore, from the Irish *Sídhe Mór*, meaning the 'Big Fairy Mound'.

Giving a name to the people in the collective or national sense won't make things as easy as naming the key characters in this story would. There aren't that many of them, however, and you'll come to know them well enough. As we go along, you'll find that they reveal their personalities in the way they carried out their work.

'The Spirits of Light' were indeed concerned with light. The later Celts regulated their calendar by the moon,[1] mainly because the lunar rhythm is easy to observe. The moon even obligingly changes its shape in a regular sequence. Its rhythm also seems to be in intimate sympathy with the fundamental feminine pendulum.

In folklore, the moon is essentially a feminine entity, whereas the sun is essentially male. Compared with the cool reserve of the nightly moon, the sun is brash, hot and aggressive. Its imperious face cannot be looked at directly. Its passionate expenditure of energy on all living things peaks and then wanes, its powerful fires dwindling to the golden glow of winter. It seems to age and become tired. Rising late and laboriously crawling low across the horizon, the elderly sun goes very early to its winter bed.

What if it died?

The builders of Newgrange were obsessed with monitoring the midwinter dawn. It's the most difficult of all observations to make. It's also the most important. The world would be in dire trouble if the sun's fire was to go out altogether. It was a time of high anxiety. Special techniques are required in order to view the annual resurgence of the weak, but still potent, sun.

Fifty-two centuries ago, civilised people were probably much the same as they are today. In the greater scheme of things, it's not really that long ago. Societies that had developed to the same extent as the Solasídhe would probably have had a lot in common with modern civilisation.

Human nature, if it changes at all, does so very slowly. It certainly wouldn't have changed very much in the short space of 50 centuries. Technologically, the people of the time would have been primitive, though 'primitive' is a relative term, of course; to some, last year's model of computer is primitive. Some say we are socially primitive. You'll soon see that, socially and philosophically, the Solasídhe were at least our equal.

They obviously had a strong desire to understand their situation, just as we do today. The ultra-modern thinker, cosmologist and Big Bang theorist, Stephen Hawking, says:

> Ever since the dawn of civilisation, people have not been content to see events as unconnected and inexplicable. They have craved an understanding of the underlying order in the world. Today we still yearn to know why we are here and where we came from. Humanity's deepest desire for knowledge is justification enough for our continuing quest. And our goal is nothing less than a complete description of the universe we live in.[2]

There are innumerable illustrations in our literature on the subject of our coming and going in this life and the meaning of it all. In drawing the character of Captain Boyle in the play *Juno and the Paycock*, for instance, Seán O'Casey echoes the simplest wonderment of all people when he causes him to ruminate: 'What is the stars?...what is the stars?'

'A darlin' question,' as the Captain's friend, Joxer, remarks, 'a darlin' question.'

Unlike Captain Boyle, however, the Solasídhe would appear to have set out to answer that 'darlin' question'. And answer it they did, in their own logical way, and to their own satisfaction, at least.

By all accounts, if you look at the amount of labour and craftsmanship that went into the building of any one of the Solasídhe's structures, they were highly advanced.

They were also certainly advanced in social terms. A social framework which was capable of supporting the very concept of such sturdy schemes must have been very stable and well established. Their system of education and training must also have been of a high order of efficiency because of the great numbers of these huge structures that were built.

They had developed their engineering techniques to a very high degree of proficiency as well. Given the huge number of their structures that have survived, intact, all over Europe, how many more of their buildings must have succumbed to outside influences in the intervening centuries? The Solasídhe were obviously constructing them as a regular, almost commonplace feature of their society.

Even today, a high degree of skill in planning and management would be required to achieve the same results. And it would be seen as an economically unsustainable waste, even today, if all that effort was to result in just a useless pile of rocks. There must have been some tangible return for the effort. Considering the size of the effort, the return must have been substantial.

The huge boulders that they used weigh just as much today as they did 52 centuries ago. They don't get lighter with time. They're also placed very accurately – too accurately for them to have employed oxen or other animals in the process. They most likely used oxen teams to drag them across the countryside from wherever they were found, but not for the final manoeuvring into place. For that they employed gangs of strong people.

They were very skilled at their work. There doesn't seem to have been any boulders misplaced in the entire construction of Newgrange. They don't appear to have dug any tryholes; at any rate, nothing of that nature has been remarked on. In fact, it can be shown that the whole system was so advanced and so efficient that most of the boulders were utilised at least twice, used for different purposes at different stages of the construction.

It was thought at one time that the great slabs that roof the alcoves in the chamber had come from another building.[3] What gave rise to this speculation was the fact that the slabs could clearly be seen to have been decorated *before* they had been put in place. An unknown amount of the incised spirals and loops obviously lay hidden by the supporting stones on which the slabs rest.

No attempt appears to have been made to incorporate the remaining visible motifs into any sort of cohesive pattern within the chamber. Therefore, it was concluded that the decoration had been carried out by others, unconnected with Newgrange, at another site. The presumption was that the other site had been dismantled to provide material for Newgrange, and that the decoration therefore didn't belong to the later building.

It was also found during the excavation of the site that some of the kerbstones in the surrounding circle outside had also been decorated on their hidden, inner faces. The remarkable sharpness of the unweathered incisions led to the conclusion that they must have been done on site, then deliberately covered up.[4] These decorations would never have been seen again after the stones were tipped into their final positions unless the whole structure was dismantled. The same applies to the half-hidden slabs in the chamber.

This doesn't appear to fit in with the Solasídhe's obvious intentions. As far as they were concerned, the stones were there to stay, which means that the so-called 'decoration' was either carved in the wrong place on the stones, or else it wasn't decoration at all.

Considering the planning skills which they display in other areas, it would seem to be highly out of character for the Master Builders to make such fundamental errors. Decorating the slabs in the wrong place and decorating the faces of boulders which they knew would subsequently be hidden is definitely not their style.

I think it's probably fair to say that it was not, and was never intended to be, 'decoration' at all.

Could they have been blueprint plans? It was proposed[5] at one time that the famous triple spiral carved into one of the stones in the chamber was a blueprint ground plan of the building.[6]

Perhaps it is, but I don't believe that the other carvings are blueprints.

The Solasídhe were known sun worshippers, and the sun was obviously very important to them. What isn't so obvious is that they found the whole of what we now call the solar system just as interesting. We know that this is true because of the huge number of other structures that are aligned with other planetary bodies.

Newgrange isn't the only Neolithic calendar page lying around on the landscape. The remainder of the sun's movement along the horizon as far as the standstill on midsummer morning and back to midwinter again can't be observed from Newgrange.

Because the building is aligned so precisely, the maximum number of sunrises that can penetrate the full depth of the passage, according to Professor O'Kelly, is 15[7], that is, 'for about a week before and a week after 21 December.' Martin Brennan, on the other hand, has observed the first chink of light entering the chamber, momentarily, 11 days before the solstice, for a total of 22.[8] For the purpose of discussion, let's settle for this greater number. What about the remaining 343 sunrises? And what about the movements of all the other heavenly bodies? How were they all to be observed?

Obviously each megalithic observatory, if you accept that that's what they are, could usually be aligned with only a small amount of movement of one heavenly body. Therefore, there had to be many different mounds aligned with not just the solar, but with all the lunar and stellar positions of note as well. That's if you believe, as I do, that the Solasídhe's intention was to keep track of the rest of the calendar.

In the immediate vicinity of Newgrange, for instance, there are over 40 sites still visible. Over half of the remaining visible specimens consist of chambered structures, some of which are still standing. They're mostly far smaller versions of Newgrange, indeed, much like scale models. Is it possible that that's exactly what they were? They're all equipped with correspondingly shorter passages, and all the passages are orientated in different directions.

Professor O'Kelly suspected that there were many more sites at Newgrange, all signs of which have been obliterated.[9] Since half of those remaining are aligned to different heavenly happenings, it can reasonably be supposed that a good proportion of the obliterated ones were also aligned. There would have been so many different alignments that the necessary observations cannot have been just an intermittent or seasonal occupation.

One of the more prominent researchers in this area is Martin Brennan, who immersed himself for many years in the subject of the designs on the stones in a search for the key to their meaning. His field exploits included staying late nights in the inner chambers of various Solasídhe structures to capture the light beams of the various lunar orientations on film. Along the way, he provided a wealth of information. Brennan's investigations clearly show that these orientations weren't accidental. Far from it.

There was a tremendous amount of Solasídhe activity going on in the Boyne Valley back then, and I believe that very little of it had to do with burying the dead. It would be more correct to refer to the area not as a cemetery, but as the world's first University of Astronomy.

In the immediate vicinity of Newgrange alone, there would have to have been dozens of observations made every day – and every night, too.

It stands to reason that the Solasídhe wouldn't have relied on solitary observations at each site. In most cases, the particular event to be observed wouldn't recur for an entire year, which means that the Solasídhe must have inevitably developed a system of specialists, with their attendant students or apprentices. The whole team had to be involved in making multiple cross-referencing observations.

Specialisation inevitably would have arisen because of the schedule of daily events. The difference in style and technique between day and night observations created two initial logical categories. The difference in style between sunrise and sunset observations produced another. Moonrise and moonset produced a further matching pair of dedicated specialist observer teams, and so on. There are so many different solar solstices and equinoxes, risings and settings, lunar waxings and wanings, stellar motions and comets' comings and goings to be continually monitored that just one observer couldn't possibly have managed them all.

The whole purpose in making all these observations was to monitor, record and keep track of the heavenly movements. But why would they have wanted to record the heavens? For the very simple reason that, just like us, they wanted to know what was happening in their world. The Solasídhe weren't striving after anything other than the reassurance that the rhythm of life was continuing safely on its predictable course.

Their apparent methodology was to build permanent calendrical observatories at suitable sites. Since the Solasídhe had no iron, as far as we know, and therefore no magnets and consequently no compasses, they were therefore incapable of transferring their observation results from site to site. Each new structure had to be surveyed afresh for the purposes of accurate orientation.

A great deal of modern thought has been expended in putting forth a timeframe for the construction phase of Newgrange. Various widely differing estimates have been made, not only about the length of time taken, but about the amount of effort and material that would have been required to complete the project.[10]

However, I believe that it was the *system* that was more important than the amount of time it took to complete. The system of masters and apprentices continuously observing the heavenly phenomena from generation to generation was bigger than any one individual's ambitions. This rigid system also ensured that their society developed and changed very slowly.

That's why Newgrange was basically just another winter solstice observatory. It was nothing out of the ordinary. As far as the building system was concerned, that is; the basic structure was no different from hundreds of others. The Solasídhe Master Builders had become experts at all the construction techniques available to them at their level of technology by the time they came to build Newgrange.

What made it unique was the very small but important difference between it and all the others that had been built previously – the roof-box.

7

MASTERS OF OBSERVATION

The sunrise appears to move backwards and forwards on the horizon between the positions of midwinter and midsummer, but it doesn't appear to do so at a constant rate. Instead, it appears to accelerate at different rates from one standstill, or solstice position, with different rates of deceleration as it approaches the next. As it approaches the winter solstice it seems to slow to a crawl.

In fact, the sun's progress along the horizon has slowed down to such an extent as it approaches the winter standstill that the difference in movement between one sunrise and the next is less than the diameter of the solar disc. It is therefore very difficult to observe the day of actual standstill without the use of a mechanism such as that built into the structure of Newgrange.

The sun penetrates to the back of the chamber at Newgrange for a number of days before and after the winter solstice. This fact has given rise to the oft-repeated but mistaken notion that the orientation is therefore not very accurate. On the contrary, the dimensions of the passage and chamber, as well as the roof-box, are carefully calculated to achieve exactly that effect.

By means of this cleverly thought out mechanism, the Solasídhe charted the sun's progress every morning (weather permitting) for at least a week on either side of the standstill. The beam of light was projected like a laser for a distance of 25 metres to the back wall of the chamber. It was the observation of the fine differences in the position of the light in the chamber from one dawn to the next over a period of two weeks that enabled the Solasídhe to pronounce the solstice with supreme accuracy.

What they were actually doing, in simple terms, was magnifying the small differences in the position of the sun by projecting it through the aperture. You can illustrate the effect yourself by shining a torch through a small slit cut in the end of a cardboard box. Any small movement of the torch will be greatly magnified where the beam strikes the inside of the box. The bigger the box, the greater the effect will be.

By means of this magnification process, the Solasídhe could clearly see when the sun had progressed to its limit of travel and then stood still before resuming its travels in the opposite direction along the horizon.

And if it was cloudy one or two mornings, what harm? As long as the light coincided with the calibrations from previous years when it was projected in the chamber the following day, or the day after, that was good enough.

It's interesting to note that the 'halcyon days' of the much later Greek civilisation refers to a fortnight of calm weather that the Greeks had observed as occurring around the time of the winter solstice. Calm weather usually means cloudless weather, which means clear skies for observations. Is it really likely that the Solasídhe would have gone to all that trouble if the weather was going to be a wash-out every year? Professor O'Kelly himself reported, with some surprise, that he had been able to observe the light show at Newgrange on one or more days around the solstice every year for 11 consecutive years.

Besides the obvious contrasts in technology, there are many other relevant differences that exist between those times and the present, such as the state of the air. Compared to our industrially polluted environment, how much more clearly would the Solasídhe have been able to see and record the motion of the heavens? The absence of city lights would have greatly enhanced their night-time powers of observation as well.

There's one very definite conclusion that can be made, however, concerning the Solasídhe's use of sunlight.

There are literally thousands of megalithic structures besides Newgrange remaining standing all over Europe, including the 1,400 estimated to remain in Ireland alone. France claims to have over 6,000, some allegedly older than Newgrange. Some have been calibrated to different periods spanning thousands of years. The types similar to Newgrange range in size from that of a dog kennel to a cathedral; one group,[1] in France, consists of 11 cathedral-sized structures built side by side under one artificial mountain.

Despite the large number of surviving structures, many more are estimated as having been destroyed for various reasons like farming, urban development, road building and similar activities which require large amounts of stone.

The French quarrying contractor who discovered the 11 complete Newgrange-type chambers, for instance, had acquired what everyone thought was a small hill. He purchased it for the convenient road-repairing-sized stones known to be contained in it. (Remember our own Mr Campbell in 1699?) Unfortunately, on this occasion, the truth was only discovered after a bulldozer had broken into and destroyed some of the chambers.[2]

All the surviving Newgrange-type structures contain a long passage and chamber, exactly as at Newgrange, and they're all, without exception, aligned with at least one heavenly phenomenon.

The fact that so many mounds were accurately aligned over such a long period means that the early surveyors must have solved the problem of blindness.

You'll go permanently blind should you attempt to observe the sun's disc directly, even for a short period of time. Even at midwinter, what appears to be the watery golden light of the rising sun is powerful enough to blind the persistent observer. The first signs of this happening will be when the sun's disc appears to dance around the sky, and sometimes appear to advance and recede rapidly, changing colour all the time. To avoid this problem, observations must be made indirectly.

The simplest form of indirect solar observation can be made with sticks stuck in the ground, to cause shadows. But since it probably took many years of observations for the Solasídhe to be certain of an alignment, a more permanent weather- and vandal-proof method would have been required, as it would have been vital to make the observations from exactly the same place every year.

You could achieve this very simply by using a tree and observing the shadow cast by it – that is, if the tree was obliging enough to grow in the right place. The further from the tree that you calibrate the fall of the shadow, the more accurate the observations should be. Unfortunately, the shadow isn't really all that sharply defined; in fact, it appears to have a blurred edge, called the penumbra, which gets less and less distinct the further you go from the tree.

Besides the inevitable guesswork that this will cause from year to year, the growth rate of the tree will very soon make nonsense of your observations. As well as that, there's very little chance of your observation markers remaining in place from year to year.

The most efficient method of making this very precise observation is exactly as the Solasídhe did it: what more permanent observation platform could be found than a big boulder? But you can't push sticks into a boulder. The answer is to first chip a little hollow into the boulder, then stand a little stone in it.

Now, not only do you have shadows, but you can also bring the little stone away with you, for safekeeping. You might even drill a hole through your little observation stone so you can string it and hang it around your neck. And what will happen the next time you set it in its socket for an observation? You'll get a streak of light through the perforation, right across the surface of the boulder.

It's a scale model of what happens at Newgrange.

You'll find, just as the Solasídhe did, that observations made in this manner are much more accurate than the old shadow system. The position of the narrow streak of light can be marked much more easily and accurately than that of a shadow. The potential for error in marking a shadow is greatly magnified by the fact that it isn't actually a sharply defined image. Secondly, would the observer, or perhaps a new observer, remember from year to year which side of the shadow was to be marked?

The lack of a magnetic compass meant that each of the Neolithic structures had to be laboriously aligned from a new set of observations made at that site. The most efficient method was then, as it would be today, to make the observations across a circle of large boulders. The same boulders, with astute Solasídhe planning, will eventually be reused as the retaining wall for the finished observatory.

Making the observations across a circle produces two reference points aligned with any event happening on the horizon. The same basic sort of technology would be utilised much, much later to achieve a different, more deadly purpose with the development of gun sights.

Presumably, a suitably flat surface on the boulder was first aligned with the horizon. The second boulder, again equipped with a suitably flat plane, was aligned with the first one, so that both flat surfaces aligned with the horizon.

Hollows chipped, picked or otherwise worn into the flat tops of these boulders served as location sockets for a variety of observation implements, probably small, finger-sized posts made of bone, wood, antler or perhaps clay.

The procedure consisted of placing a device in a chosen socket to serve as a fore-sight on the boulder nearest the horizon. As the sun rose (or whatever other heavenly activity began) the back-sight device was moved around on its boulder until it lined up with the fore-sight and the item being observed. The position of the back-sight was then marked permanently, probably with a socket to receive it at the same time the following year.

After the observations were made, the portable implements were removed and kept safe until required for the next day's sighting.

The stability of such a system served to prevent the observations from being disturbed from year to year. As the specialists became more expert, they needed to make their observations on fewer stones in the circle, perhaps as few as two or three, as they became familiar with the expected positions of the heavenly bodies.

In the beginning, simple, unperforated sighting devices were used and the observations made with the cast shadows. The invention of the perforated sighting device had a profound effect. Not only did it immediately improve the accuracy of the observations, but it also meant that only one platform would be required.

The perforation doubled the effectiveness of the sighting device, since it changed the point on the horizon from being a target at which to aim into becoming a fore-sight. The second sighting device was now redundant. Now all the observer had to do to make an accurate observation was to aim the perforated sight at the relevant point on the horizon. As the sun rose, the resultant streak of light was fine tuned to perfection by rotating the sight until the streak of light was fully sharp and as narrow as possible.

When a satisfactory alignment had been established for the proposed observatory, the boulders, complete with observers' records carved into them, were unceremoniously tipped up on edge, into their final resting places in the kerb.

At one time it was proposed that the stones had been used elsewhere, as gravestones, and that consequently the carvings bore no relevance to Newgrange.[3] On the contrary, the carvings were very much a part – and a very important part – of the structure, in two ways: once as observation platforms, and then as members of the retaining kerb. But there was absolutely no significance whatsoever attached to the hiding of the carved symbols. They were merely finished with, redundant.

Incidentally, every time archaeologists dig out a megalithic mound, they find hoards of little round-ended stones with holes through them, which they class, reasonably enough because of obvious wear marks, as pendants. Nineteenth-century archaeologists would probably have called them 'perforated miniliths', following suit with their system of classification.

All, that is, except for a beautifully carved and decorated white flint with a perfectly regular perforation, which was found during the excavations at Knowth, the neighbouring site to Newgrange. This most unusual one, it was decided, was a 'ceremonial mace-head'.[4]

Which, of course, it could well have been. After all, it's somewhat bigger than usual. And the other ones could well have been pendants – I believe that the little pebbles did in fact spend most of their time as pendants. But I also believe that they were regularly unstrung and employed in their more important role as aperture 'sights'.

The accuracy of such sights relies on the fact that the human eye will automatically place a target in the centre of a circular aperture. Because the certainty of blindness meant that the solar observations must be made indirectly and because the observation of shadows cast by a standing object isn't very satisfactory, some other system of observation must have been developed by the Solasídhe. I am suggesting that an aperture sighting system solves both of those problems. I am further suggesting that the empiric development of such a system is a simple logical progression. The Solasídhe engineers weren't theorists. They were experts in the true sense of the word. They developed their techniques very slowly, but surely, by trial and error.

And if all that's true, then the so-called 'cup-marks' so liberally dotted around and amongst the incised 'designs' on the stones must be the matching observation sockets in which the perforated stones were placed. (At last count, however, something like 27 different theories have already been offered to explain these 'cup-marks'.)

You can probably visualise the scene any winter morning in the cold and misty pre-dawn on the bare hillside above the bend of the Boyne: the Master Builder standing there, alone, on the site chosen for the high-tech building that would become known as Newgrange.

The Master Forester has already cleared the trees from the hilltop, and with the aid of the Master Farmer's labourers has also stripped the turf from outside the loose circle of boulders, in a wide swathe down the hill towards the river.

The sods of turf are stockpiled at the top of the hill, ready to be used as packing under the boulders when they come to be placed in their final positions, and as stabilising layers in the cairn which would be finally heaped up over the completed structure.

The dark shale exposed by this operation gleams wetly in the mist. The apprentice observers are all kneeling close to one of the boulders in the circle near the top of the hill. Each of them has placed a perforated pebble in a small hollow on the top of the boulder.

At the direction of the Master Observer, they carefully align the apertures on the chosen target on the horizon. The Master knows from experience exactly where to expect the sun to appear.

As the first rim of the sun peeps over the horizon, they all lean over their respective stones, pulling their cloaks up over their heads, draping them over their pebbles, being careful not to block the aperture.

On the command of the Master, who calls for a sequence of observations according to the position of the sun's disc as it clears the horizon, they each in turn mark the position of the streak of light from the aperture on their sighting stone. They use a variety of markers – lumps of chalk, bits of bone and sharp edges of flint. They then spend the morning making the successful marks more permanent. The Master Observer compares the results with previous observations. Inevitably, some of them have got it wrong. They will have to wait another year to try again.

When sufficient observations are made for the Master Builder to begin, one of the first operations carried out is to tip the circle of boulders up on edge, butting each one against the next, forming a retaining wall for the site. The redundant observations carved into the boulders won't be seen again for 5,000 years, not until Professor O'Kelly uncovers them during his restoration of the site.

Which brings us back to the roof slab in the chamber, the one that had been 'decorated' before it was placed in its final position. If you accept that the so-called 'decoration' on the boulders of the outer kerb is in actual fact the record of sunrises and other observations, then obviously the roof slab had been used as an observation platform as well. After all, it carries exactly the same type of incised markings as the others.

But why wasn't it incorporated into the outer circle of kerbstones? The answer to that question has to do with the expert quantity surveying skills displayed by the Solasídhe.

Presumably the Master Observer required observations to be recorded of the angle of elevation of the sun to correlate with the horizontal, or azimuth, observations. Without such three-dimensional computations, it would not be possible to arrive at the accuracy of alignment which the Solasídhe did in fact achieve.

The horizon to the south-east is slightly higher than the roof-box at Newgrange, and the floor of the chamber is slightly lower than the roof-box. It's also evident that the entire disc of the sun has to rise above the horizon before its rays can fully enter the roof-box, which means that the angle of the rays is slightly downward, and not horizontal, as is often supposed.[5]

In order to observe and record the angle of its meeting with what was to become the floor of the chamber, it was necessary for a vertical face of a slab to be orientated, 'edge-on' to the sunrise. The chosen boulder had to be very carefully aligned with the solstice sunrise so that its flat face was exactly parallel with the path of the light. At the same time, it had to be perfectly vertical.

Not an easy task.

This operation is the most complicated of all the construction techniques employed at Newgrange. More than that, it's the key which is critical to unlocking the whole purpose of the structure.

If the vertical observation slab is only infinitesimally out of line in either axis, the results will be unacceptably poor. Obviously the Solasídhe engineers had mastered the principle of the plumb-bob, because that's the only feasible mechanism by which they could have succeeded in this complicated and delicate manoeuvre.

On the drawing made by Will Jones, Edward Lhwyd's draughtsman in 1699 (Lhwyd was one of the first people to investigate and record the physical dimensions of Newgrange), there's a representation of an object which had been found lying, according to Jones, 'in ye right hand cistern, under ye bason above mentioned.' The notes on the drawing go on to describe the object: 'a stone wrought in the form of a cone, half a yard long & about 20 inches in the girth, having a small hole at ye big end.'

In their efforts to modify this object so as to fit with the theory that it was a 'ceremonial mace-head', some commentators[6] argued that Jones must have been mistaken, that the hole must have been in the other end. Even though I run the risk of being accused of suiting my own purpose, I can't find any reason to suggest that Jones, a professional draughtsman, couldn't tell one end from the other. Even today, you won't better Jones's description of a general purpose, non-metallic plumb-bob.

If the Solasídhe had arrived at the plumb-bob, then it's almost certain that they had also mastered the principle of the shear-legs. Suspending a plumb-bob from the apex of a shear-legs is still the classic engineering solution for many problems associated with positioning objects accurately, especially during building construction. The two go together, hand in hand, as a fundamental engineering duo.

If all that's true, and it seems very probable that it is, then the Solasídhe engineers were very likely to have taken the next logical step. They would have realised, sooner rather than later in the construction phase, that they could make life a lot easier for themselves if they were to suspend the chosen boulder from the shear-legs.

Using the plumb-bob to check the adjustments and by dint of trial and error, shifting rope slings back and forth, they soon discovered that they could get the vertical alignment just right. After that, the rest of the job was simple. By suspending the boulder just clear of the floor, all that was required was fingertip pressure to achieve a superbly accurate azimuth alignment of the huge stone.

The same system of perforated sighting stones placed in appropriate hollows cut into the vertical face of the boulder provided a very accurate record of the sun's angle with the site. Obviously, since the observation platform was in the vertical, the sighting stones were held in place with one hand (or with somebody else's hand), and the other hand was used for marking the streak of light.

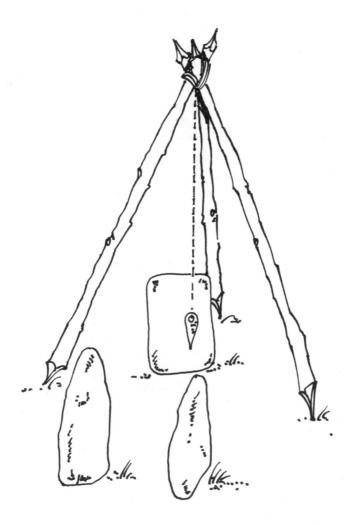

ELEVATION STONE AND PLUMB-BOB

When these observations had been scored or scraped into the vertical face of the standing stone over a number of seasons, it, too, bore all the hallmarks of the observer's craft.

But what then?

Obviously the best position for such a standing stone was directly in the path of the light beam. Therefore it had to be removed when the observations were complete, otherwise it would obstruct the shaft of sunlight at the time of the solstice. The very purpose for which the structure was built in the first place would be nullified if it remained standing in the passage.

It had to go, but the superb planning of the structure meant that it didn't have to travel very far – it went straight up into the roof, hauled up with the aid of the shear-legs from which it had originally been suspended.

Very neat. Very efficient. Very Solasídhe.

And who cares whether the designs, decoration or whatever you want to call the observer's records were covered up or not? They had done their job and were of no further use. They were redundant. But they hadn't been cannibalised from another structure – they belong to Newgrange.

Presumably the boulders were used by a number of specialists, in which case the observations had to be differentiated from each other. Standardisation of the symbols for the different schools of observation had to have been introduced to avoid total confusion.

It seems reasonable to suppose that the different schools had different sizes or types of sighting stones as well. Perhaps they had a system of grading by the type of stone from which they were fashioned. They were probably distinctive badges of office, recognisable to the hierarchy of Solasídhe Professors of Astronomy.

Could the beautiful white stone, the exquisitely carved 'ceremonial mace-head' found at Knowth, have been the Master Observer's prized possession, a personal sighting stone, the symbol of exalted office? Who knows?

The development of a system such as I have described ensured that all the observations were made from exactly the same position from year to year, and also ensured that the observations themselves were recorded with the utmost accuracy. Among the other advantages that such a system offered the Solasídhe observers is that they were able to keep their knowledge safe from the gaze of the common people.

Once they had removed the sighting stones, which then reverted to being inconsequential personal adornments, there was nothing left to give the secret away. All that remained in view for the casual passer-by were some enigmatic carvings which were probably embellished as 'ornament' in order to further conceal their true purpose.

It was, after all, the high technology of their time, and they no doubt preferred to keep the secrets of its operation to a select few, literally keeping their knowledge close to their chests – hanging on a string around their necks.

Yet think what consternation there would have been if an observer had lost one of the precious sighting stones! In addition, the custodians of this knowledge couldn't afford to have the key to their technology fall into the wrong hands. Security would have been paramount even then, which may be why they buried so many of the little pebbles under the basin stones inside the structures.

Now that we have outlined the methods used by the Solasídhe to chart the movements of the heavens, you'll find it much easier to understand what I have found that makes Newgrange doubly unique.

Yes, it's a superb example of the monumental calendar-maker's craft. Yes, it does accurately chart the very fine movements of the sun at the turn of the year. But I believe it's also much more than that. I believe it's a quantum leap in the development of society, equivalent in its own way, perhaps, to the invention of the steam engine, the aeroplane or the computer.

Certainly, the knowledge that the year was turning was of immense value to a civilisation newly dependent on agriculture, as the timing of crop planting was crucial for a successful harvest.

But it was also a reassurance that everything was under control, that mankind was in complete command of the situation; or more precisely, that everything was under the control of a few men or, perhaps, women.

Because control is what it was all about. It probably didn't start out that way, but inevitably, human nature being what it is, the Solasídhe soon discovered that the ones who have knowledge also have power.

8

THE CONSTRUCTION

The Solasídhe had focused on the sun as being the most important thing in their daily life, and they set out to discover what made it tick. Now, catching a sunbeam is an altogether different proposition to catching an animal for the slaughter or hooking a fish from the river. Each of these different pursuits requires a very different type of knowledge.

But they all have something in common: each technique had to be learned empirically, by trial and error, experiment and experience. By the time they came to build Newgrange, the Solasídhe had refined and polished their light-catching techniques to a very high order of efficiency.

Now that you have some idea of what the Solasídhe were doing and, more importantly, *how* they were doing it, let's go back to the little hill above the Boyne and observe how they proceeded with the construction.

Just by way of diversion, ask yourself how difficult it would be to build a long passage so as to align it accurately with a particular solar event, given the benefit of today's technology. Let's say you wanted to have it occur on your birthday, at mid-day. All you would need is a small cement mixer, a supply of building blocks, a couple of tonnes of sand, aggregate, cement and mortar, a brickie with a couple of labourers armed with picks and shovels, supervised by a surveyor with a compass, theodolite and almanac of solar declinations.

About a week's work is all it would take to have your own personal birthday observatory in place – a couple of days making observations, preparing the site and erecting the passage and chamber; a couple more days for the roofing; one full day piling up the covering mound, with maybe another day spent covering the south side in broken pieces of white quartz.

The same task, 52 centuries ago, must have been a very daunting prospect for the Solasídhe Master Builder. Not only was there no metal in those times, but there was no cement either. Most of what they built was composed of dry stone, with no bonding of any kind.

More significantly, the Solasídhe had apparently not yet discovered the techniques of quarrying or hewing stone.[1] All the large stones used in the building of Newgrange were weathered, and had been dragged or otherwise transported to the site, untreated in any way, from wherever they had been found lying on the landscape.

But the builders had a trick or two up their sleeves to compensate for the lack of modern materials and technology. One of the Solasídhe's lesser but nevertheless remarkable skills uncovered during the excavation was the clever practice of cutting grooves on the stones to lead rainwater away from the interior passage and chamber. Now, what is that – sophisticated architectural detail, or a sound grasp of gravity, fluid dynamics and surface levelling?

Just as the Solasídhe builders had done, a modern contractor would soon discover that when dealing with light, it displays certain unique characteristics. For one thing, it always travels in a straight line. That may not sound earth-shattering to us today, but to the Solasídhe, it meant one very important thing – they could make very fine and very accurate adjustments to a beam of light with just the merest edge of a stone.

It didn't have to be the whole profile of the stone, just part of it, and they found that they didn't have to do all the adjustment at the one place, either – a bit here, another bit further on. Any beam of sunlight, or indeed moonlight and starlight, too, that had been captured between two standing stones could be sculpted into any desired shape.

Suddenly, every great lump of rock became a precision instrument. It only had to be a small part of the rock which performed this precision light-sculpting; the remainder of the stone was redundant, unless it had been designed to double as part of the structure.

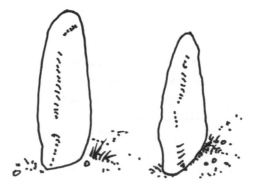

THE PILLARS

Martin Brennan's field work clearly demonstrated that the Solasídhe had developed this method of light-sculpting to a very high level of precision. The practice of confining, shaping and projecting light beams was central to their method of observation of the heavens and it wasn't by any means unique to Newgrange. The practice was apparently well established[2] by the time they came to build this, the showpiece of the Solasídhe's technology.

Although Newgrange is certainly unique, it wasn't by any means a prototype, at least not a prototype of the building technique. As we proceed, you'll notice that all of the light-sculpting stones at Newgrange, both vertical and horizontal, are also incorporated as load-bearing components into the structure. Everything is used at least twice. It becomes apparent that Newgrange is very sophisticated, not only in its planning, but in every small detail of its construction. What's also apparent is that it wasn't designed by committee. When you see how Newgrange actually works, you'll realise that it bears all the hallmarks of individual genius. The stunning special effect for which it was created all that time ago must have been of such radical novelty that no committee could possibly have conceived it.

If you have a creative project that you want organised, managed and put into effect, then you need a committee, but committees aren't good at the creative process. There's an old adage that the camel is a horse designed by a committee.[3] The Solasídhe may well have had committees – who knows? – but as far as I can see, the original designer of Newgrange was quite obviously a genius.

The first and most important of the four clues to our genius's master plan is the so-called roof-box. Everything else is dependent upon its accuracy, and its accuracy is in turn dependent upon the precision with which the primary observations were carried out at the site.

The second clue is bound up, first of all, in the choice of the corbelling method for the construction of the chamber roof, and secondly, in the special form taken by the corbelling. Corbelling is a primitive architectural technique of roofing over an open space with stone slabs. In simple terms, a succession of flat stone slabs is laid one over the other, each course projecting beyond or oversailing the one below, much like a flight of steps. Starting from opposite sides of the space to be roofed over, the corbelling eventually meets in the centre under one final capstone.

The Master Builder employed a highly sophisticated variation[4] of the corbelling technique in roofing the chamber in Newgrange, a variation that we will examine in detail later on.

Clue number three is found, firstly, in the positioning of the capstone of that corbelling and, secondly, in the procedures necessary for it to arrive in that position.

The fourth clue is in the series of curves apparent in the construction of the narrow passage. Previous commentators have mentioned that there are two;[5] I see twice that number. The third curve in the passage isn't readily apparent to the observer of the finished structure; it only became apparent to me as I built the model. That's because it's a reflex curve, joining the two curves already mentioned. The fourth curve of stones isn't readily apparent, either; it's formed by the stones supporting the original capstone of the entrance structure. This last curve (which was actually the first to be built) isn't as pronounced as the other three, but nevertheless, it's a curve.

When these four clues are put together in the right order, the body of evidence that they represent will lead you to a realisation of just what a true genius the Solasídhe Master Builder was.

There are many other secondary clues, mainly to do with the choice of site, all of which seem to support the main conclusion. These exterior, supporting pieces of evidence are contained in the physical topography of the surrounding terrain. Nevertheless, the main conclusion can be arrived at solely from an examination of the four mechanical clues contained in the structure of the building.

We will return to the exterior clues later, after we have put the four main items in order.

First, the all-important roof-box.

It's a simple truth that the longer and narrower a passage in a Solasídhe structure, the fewer the number of sunrises that can penetrate its depths. And since they obviously felt that the best place to catch the sunrise is on a hilltop, another limiting factor enters the picture: the longer the passage grows, the further the slope falls away until the entrance is too far downhill to receive the incoming light. It falls away so far that the doorway has to be even higher than the tallest stones that you can find in order for the dawn's early light to continue to penetrate to the full depth of the structure.

One obvious answer would be to level the site. That would not have been a huge task, given the abundance of labour available. But it wasn't the answer at Newgrange. The far simpler and more elegant solution, and probably another first for early Irish architecture, was to build a second storey and let the light in through a first-floor window.

So why, you might ask, did the Master Builder continue the passage onwards, downhill, beyond the upstairs window, or roof-box? What was the purpose, you might further ask, since the passage at this point was already seriously out of alignment with the sunrise?

In fact, the passage extends so far downhill that the midwinter sunrise only penetrates about halfway into it; meanwhile, the sun's rays have entered the upstairs window and laser-beamed straight to the back wall of the chamber, exactly as was intended. So what, you might ask, is the purpose of the extra length of seemingly useless passage?

Actually, it wasn't built that way at all.

One thing of enormous significance that Professor O'Kelly was able to determine as he dismantled the structure was the strange fact that the first part of the passage, which includes the entrance and roof-box, had been built separately[6] from the corbelled chamber. In fact, the chamber and the entrance had been built as completely separate, free-standing sub-structures.

The significance of that discovery is that the midwinter alignment between the two sub-structures had obviously been established at the outset, as the very first objective of the master plan. So what must the sequence of building have been if that was the case?

We had left the Master Observer with the apprentices on the hill, making their final observations. No construction had yet been started. The reason for that, as we now know, was that the vital vertical observations had to be completed before any building could proceed, which means that a very substantial shear-legs had to have been erected at the top of the hill and the vertical observation stone positioned directly underneath it. We know that this stone would eventually become redundant, as soon as the elevation of the midwinter sun had been satisfactorily established, and would be reused in the roof of the yet-to-be-built chamber.

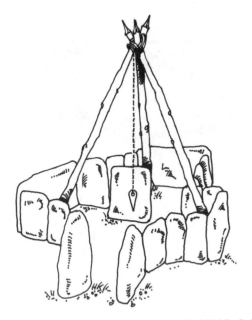

ELEVATION STONE AND PLUMB-BOB

It's entirely reasonable to presume that they left the shear-legs in place, at least until the chamber walls were ready to receive the observation stone as part of the roof. What would be the point in dismantling the shear-legs, only to have to re-erect it shortly afterwards?

But they wouldn't have removed the vertical observation stone until the required angle of elevation of the midwinter sun had been properly established, which means that the roof-box had to have been constructed before the vertical stone was removed. Otherwise, the correct alignment between the two component sub-structures could not have been established.

It follows that the very essence of the whole structure – the roof-box, our first clue – was the very first part of the structure to be completed.

ENTRANCE WITH ROOF-BOX

Imagine what the structure would look like at this point if the Solasídhe builders were to abandon the site. A huge, flat stone supported by half a dozen standing stones sounds to me very like a dolmen, or, more properly, a 'portal tomb', as they have been reclassified. Could it be that at least some of the portal tombs are the beginnings, or perhaps the remains, of Newgrange-type structures?

Meanwhile, we can now say for certain that the front part of the passage – carrying the roof-box – was fully completed before the chamber was even half-built. The Solasídhe obviously considered it so important that they ensured its correct positioning and alignment before they commenced the passage construction phase. We can also say one other very significant and probably very surprising thing: the shape of the chamber was dictated by the presence of the shear-legs. It would appear to follow logically that the shear-legs was erected first, and the chamber built around the whole apparatus.

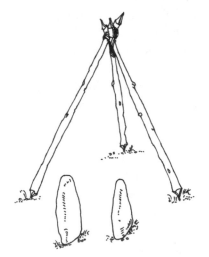

THE PILLARS AND SHEAR-LEGS

The scale model shows this very clearly. The standing stones of the chamber appear to have been set in place around the feet of the shear-legs, encroaching between the legs of the tripod mechanism to form crude pillars. It was the positioning of the feet of the shear-legs which also explains the off-setting of the alcoves in the chamber. I have not seen any explanations offered for this off-setting, although it has been well noted. I don't think that the Solasídhe were too concerned about the orderliness of the layout; for them, it was more important that the construction worked properly.

A brief explanation of the shear-legs principle will help clarify things. The minimum number of legs for an effective shear-legs is three, where first a pair of timbers are positioned with the legs spread apart and tied loosely at the top, where they cross one another; the top of the third leg is set into the crutch that's formed as the first pair are raised towards and beyond the vertical.

The main pair of legs is then swung slowly back and forth, under finer and finer control, with a plumb-bob suspended from the apex. When the plumb-bob indicates that the apex of the apparatus is positioned vertically over the desired location, the main legs are tied off to the third, support leg.

The positioning of the feet follows logically, because, at Newgrange, the shear-legs was erected on a slope: between the chamber and the entrance, the ground falls two metres. Therefore, the foot of the third, stabilising leg had to be positioned further downhill from either of the two main legs. Its optimum position lies at right angles to the baseline of the main legs for maximum effective stability. Otherwise, the weight-lifting capacity of the apparatus would be diminished and the risk of sideways collapse increased.

For compactness and efficiency, the main legs were made to straddle the path of the incoming light. They could both have been positioned to one side of the light beam, but that would have meant that the chamber would end up being much larger, much too big, in fact, to be roofed by the corbelling method.

Another penalty clause would then be applied: the main legs would have had to swing much further from their base, at a much shallower angle with the chamber floor, in order for the arc of traverse of the apex to be positioned anywhere over the line of the incoming light beam, which was the object of the exercise, after all.

Under those circumstances, since the third leg would necessarily have to be footed downhill from the lower of the main pair, the knock-on effect would have been that the third leg would either have to have had an enormously long reach or would have been so short as to have been ineffective.

None of which would have improved the weight-lifting capacity of the apparatus. There would have been some difficulty, and not a little danger of collapse, when it came time for the vertical observation stone to be suspended and then positioned in the path of the incoming light.

The straddled positioning is in fact the most efficient in the circumstances: it allows the chamber dimensions to be as compact as possible, and at the same time allows the shear-legs to stand erect enough to be capable of supporting some considerable weight.

So, the main legs of the apparatus had to be positioned so that the foot of one leg was further downhill than the other, which meant that the alcoves, which were formed around the feet of the shear-legs, were inevitably off-set one to the other across the chamber.

And so, after a satisfactory set of observations was completed, the time came to lift the vertical stone up out of the way, into the roof. As Professor O'Kelly's excavation was able to reveal,[7] a platform composed of small, water-rolled boulders (presumably obtained from the nearby river bed) had been piled up against the standing stones, forming a stable platform on the outside of the chamber, level with the tops of the standing stones. The redundant vertical observation stone was hauled up and swung from the shear-legs out onto this platform. It was then no great hardship to push it into position to leave it resting on the tops of the standing stones, so forming a roof for the alcove below it.

ELEVATION STONE AS FIRST CORBEL

In its new position, the front edge of this stone appears to have been very close to, if not actually touching, one of the slanting shear-legs. The same is true of the roofing slabs of the other alcoves (if you accept that the north extremity of the passage is an alcove), which touch, or almost touch, the other members of the shear-legs apparatus.

The roofing slabs of the alcoves could be said to form the first courses of the corbelling of the chamber roof. But the rate of oversailing of the successive courses had to be more restrained in their reach. There were no vertical supports under them, such as those under the alcove roof slabs. However, they continue to encroach on the roof space as quickly as the technique will allow.

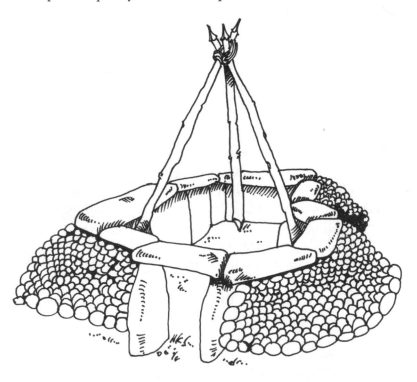

CORBELLING: PHASE 1

Anyone who has ever tried the trick of building a stairway of coins will remember this technique. With a steady hand, you add precarious pennies to the pile. Attempting the same thing six metres up using one-tonne slabs of rock instead of coins deserves more than just a round of applause. If even one of those rocks started to slip...well, I wouldn't like to be working inside the chamber at Newgrange on that particular day.

Professor O'Kelly surmised that the builders probably used horsing, or temporary, vertical support timbers, positioned under the inner edges of the corbelling slabs.[8] These timbers would most likely have been driven up against the slabs, taking their weight by means of opposed wedges hammered in under them.

It would therefore have been fairly congested in the chamber, what with the three members of the shear-legs rising at an angle between the forest of vertical horsing timbers which, in turn, would have encroached relentlessly on the remaining floor space as the corbelling progressed.

By the time it came to place the capstone, the inside of the chamber would have looked like a surrealist three-dimensional maze. None of the horsing timbers could have been removed until the tails of the corbelling slabs had all been counter-weighted on the outside of the structure.

Professor O'Kelly's investigations showed that the corbelling had indeed been stabilised, not just with counterweighting stones, but with a complete cairn of boulders.[9] The resulting cairn enclosed the chamber substructure, complete with its shear-legs, in a six-metre high conical shroud of stone.

Still concentrating on this extraordinary roof, there are two things I would like to point out. Firstly, we know that there was no difficulty in roofing over the chamber at a much lower height with a couple of large, flat slabs, similar to the ones used for the same purpose down at the entrance. Secondly, as you can readily appreciate from the description of the process, corbelling is exceptionally dangerous. For my money, if I was building the thing, it would have been the big, flat slab every time.

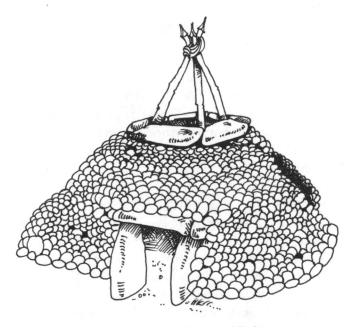

CORBELLING PHASE 2

Professor O'Kelly surmised that in the original construction of the corbelled chamber roof, the successive rounds of oversailing slabs were temporarily supported on their inner ends by vertically placed timbers, or 'horsing', fixed at floor level with opposed wedges.[10] I took up this suggestion, going so far as to paint the picture above of the interior of the chamber as a forest of horsing as the construction proceeded.

I have heard some of his peers disparage Professor O'Kelly as a converted engineer, which reflects badly on them. I cannot think of a more beneficial discipline to add to the armoury of skills necessary to the practice of archaeology than that of the oldest profession, engineering. Professor O'Kelly, possessing a modicum of engineering knowledge, was naturally intrigued as to the possible engineering methods employed in the construction of Newgrange; the same knowledge made him cautious of disturbing the extremely sophisticated roof structure. Consequently, his dissertation on the horsing procedure is born out of theory, not of evidence.

In the absence of supporting evidence, one theory is as good as the next, and I believe I have some evidence – tenuous, I accept, but evidence nevertheless – for my theory. It's in two parts, as follows.

Firstly, using simple logic, the horsing procedure would never have worked.

Professor O'Kelly did find evidence that the slabs in each course of corbelling had been tilted up slightly at their contiguous inner ends so that as they settled against the ballasting boulders piled against their outer ends, they bore against each other, forming a horizontal arch. Furthermore, the builders had laid small pieces of frangible stone on the previously laid course of corbelling. This was crushed under the weight of the new course settling on it, thereby distributing the weight more evenly – all in all, a very sophisticated piece of engineering.

So sophisticated, in fact, that it's logically inconceivable that the engineers would have employed the horsing method, the reason being that each course of corbelling had to be allowed to settle before the next course was laid. Therefore, the horsing would necessarily have been removed to facilitate the settling. Therefore, all the horsing for each course would have to have been removed simultaneously, because if just one pole remained wedged in place as the others were removed, then at the very least the integrity of the horizontal arch would be destroyed. At worst, the whole course of corbelling would come tumbling down into the chamber.

I don't believe that the sophisticated engineers who built Newgrange would persevere with such an inefficient and potentially dangerous procedure. Instead, I believe that in keeping with their obvious mastery of the technology of megalithic manipulation, they used a more typically original, elegant and sophisticated solution.

It does not stretch credulity or strain the imagination to conclude that the builders of Newgrange must have pioneered some classic engineering procedures; we have deduced that in all probability they invented the plumb-bob, the relieving arch, the shear-legs and the Spanish windlass. It's only a short step from there to the 'lost sand' solution.

I now believe that the only feasible method by which they could have built the corbelled chamber at Newgrange was to fill the chamber brim-full of dry sand, lay the slabs on the sand, ballast them on their outer edges and release a slow, controlled flow of sand down below in the chamber.

They very likely stacked baulks of timber inside the pillar stones forming the entrance to the chamber to form a retaining dam. It would not take much ingenuity to construct a chute into the centre of the chamber with a simple mechanism to initiate the release of and control the flow of the sand.

As the sand flowed from the centre of the pile, the slabs would settle equally, under control, settling perfectly every time into their horizontal arch configuration. Then the sand team refilled the chamber from the top with leather bags of sand, and the engineers started the next course.

In no time at all, a perfectly sound structure of successive courses of corbelling would be completed with this method.

The 'lost sand' technique is supposed to have been first used in Egypt for the building of the pyramids. And perhaps the pharaohs' architects did arrive at that method independently, for the simple reason that they have an abundance of sand out there.

75

But there's plenty of sand at this site, too.

In fact, Professor O'Kelly noted the existence of a 'bank of yellow clay' outside the structure, to the west of the entrance.[11] There's no great amount of detail as to its composition or its extent in the excavation report. But if it were dried in the sun, would it take on the characteristics of dry sand? What if it *is* the sand from the chamber construction phase? Wouldn't it be worth having another look?

However, let's resume our deliberations on this knotty problem of the corbelling: the Solasídhe Master Builder could have closed over the corbelling at any height over about three metres, when the first courses of corbelling had closed over the space as far as the shear-legs. They most certainly could have 'topped out' the chamber at any one of the succeeding courses of their choice above that height. In fact, they would have been able to use the one size of capstone at any one of the final five courses of corbelling.

Which inevitably leads to the question: for what purpose did the Solasídhe want the extra height? A closer inspection of the top section of corbelling reveals a very narrow, chimney-like structure. We know that the reason it survived the collapse of the outer mantle was due to the extraordinary mastery with which it was assembled. In his report, Professor O'Kelly had this to say:

> The slabs were laid with an outward slope and as the weight increased on their inner ends, these ends became tightly locked together, so that in effect, each course became a horizontal arch...the fact that the roof did not collapse during this (later) settlement shows how well built it was, and that it still stands today is a very great tribute to the builders.[12]

Incidentally, Professor O'Kelly declined the opportunity of dismantling this part of the structure in fear that it might collapse while they were working on it.[13] I wonder if in fact his real fear might not have been that for all the modern technology at his disposal, he might not have been able to put it back together again exactly as he had found it.

At any rate, he reckoned that it was good for another 5,000 years as it stood, which is a very high order of tribute to bestow on the Master Builder.

The model clearly shows that when the shear-legs was erected and after the standing stones forming the chamber walls had been placed around the feet of the apparatus, the Master Builder then proceeded to close over the chamber as quickly as the corbelling technique would allow. The result, as clearly shown by the model, meant that when the corbelling eventually met the slant of the shear-legs again, the roof was just about halfway complete.

From that point on, however, the corbelling takes on the shape of the remaining height of the shear-legs, snugly encasing the last three metres or so of the apparatus, right up to the final closing stone above its apex.

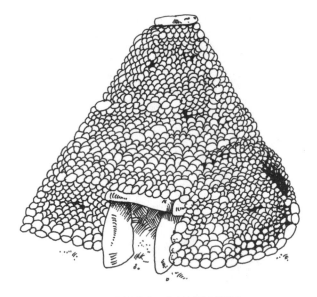

CHAMBER COMPLETE

That's the second clue.

All of which leads to another conclusion: the shear-legs was intended to remain in situ inside the completed chamber, because if it wasn't, then they would obviously have dismantled the whole rig, which would have allowed them to cap the chamber much earlier.

They could very easily have raised up the final capstone, leaving it aside in readiness, on the top of the mound, removed the shear-legs and slid the capstone into place.

The fact that they didn't is the third clue.

There isn't any evidence remaining in the building at this point in time of wooden artefacts. There might have been some indication remaining in the floor of Newgrange of previously existing timber, but that would have been obliterated by later disturbances. Perhaps some other site, so far unexcavated, will shed some light on the subject when it comes time for a properly conducted investigation. Meanwhile, we'll move on to the fourth clue.

PASSAGE PHASE 1

Only after the solar alignment between the roof-box and the separate chamber had been established was the 20 metres of passage constructed, linking the two. An intriguing feature of this phase of the construction is the series of four curves in the line of the passage. It's clear that the curves were deliberately formed and were not, as one might be tempted to surmise, the result of careless workmanship on the part of the Master Builder.

It becomes clear that the curves are a series of arcs joining up a procession of light-sculpting arches. These arches appear to have been constructed so as to gradually control and shape the sunlight into a sharp, well-defined beam. In order to achieve this effect, each of the arches is slightly off-set to the last one, and the lintel of each gets lower as they progress outwards toward the rising sun.

It seems most likely that the run of standing stones proceeded downhill from the chamber, in three curves, to link up with the entrance structure. As has already been noted, the reflex curve in the middle of the three isn't readily apparent. Neither is the fourth curve, because it's formed by the stones which form the entrance structure, which in turn supports the roof-box.

There's a gap between the third and fourth standing stones on the right-hand side of the passage as you enter. This gap had been filled in with a short run of dry stone wall, which Professor O'Kelly concluded was part of the original structure.[14] The third standing stone belongs to the entrance structure, so the fourth one is the last of the downhill run. It seems logical that if there was to be a gap, it would be at the end of the run rather than at the beginning.

The slabs roofing the passage were then laid, corbel fashion, in the opposite direction from that of the standing stones, like the steps of a flight of stairs, proceeding from the entrance to the chamber. But it's actually three flights of stairs. At two significant points, the series of steps begins again, and the starting point of each succeeding flight is the cross lintel of the light-shaping arches.

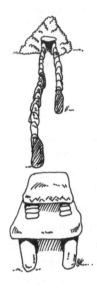

PASSAGE PHASE 2

In between each of the massive arches, the passage was lined with the equally massive standing stones, but each run of stones was carefully set in a shallow arc so as not to intrude on the shaft of light.

So, if we are to extend the logic of that procedure to the seemingly redundant fourth curve of stones, down towards the entrance, the obvious conclusion is that the entrance itself forms a light-shaping arch.

But why? How could that be?

Since the builders constructed the passage from the chamber towards the entrance, they must have been well aware of the fact that the passage at that point was seriously out of alignment with the midwinter dawn. So far out of alignment, in fact, that the sun's rays through the entrance could never have penetrated any further than halfway down the passage.

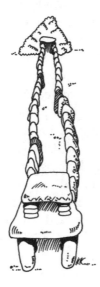

PASSAGE PHASE 3

If you stand way back in the passage and look out the entrance, you can see how far out of alignment it had become: the Boyne River is neatly framed in the doorway, about one kilometre away at the bottom of the valley. Nevertheless, from the same position you can see that the line of sight through the roof-box meets the line of the local horizon, the Red Mountain, on the south side of the river. But still the Solasídhe Master Builder seems to have persevered with the light-sculpting technique, even though it was abundantly clear that the effort was being wasted.

Incidentally, the view out the front door is somewhat restricted by the large stone lying on its side just outside the entrance. The effect is very similar to that created by the succession of reducing lintels in the passage; it's almost like looking the wrong way down a telescope at the distant river. Except for the even larger stone standing vertically further down the hill outside the entrance. It seems, somehow, to be out of sequence with all the others. It very nearly blocks the view down into the valley altogether.

Logic demands that we re-examine the situation. The question is: why does the passage continue to form a light-sculpting curve down there, right down towards the entrance? The curve at that point is beyond the position where the light coming in through the roof-box isn't just overhead height, but is actually far above the tops of the standing stones lining the passage.

The logical conclusion must therefore be that the sculpting effect of the curve in the passage entrance area had nothing at all to do with shaping the light entering through the roof-box.

In the 1:24 scale model, the shape of the light beam from the roof-box is startlingly sharp when it reaches the chamber, but the model also revealed that this phenomenon can only be observed when the passage entrance is closed up. (Those hardy people who congregate in the chamber every winter at solstice-time aren't getting their full shilling's worth: the spill of light from the passage entrance effectively reduces the magic of the light beam, preventing it from being revealed in its full clarity.)

The largest of the light-sculpting arches is the innermost one, at the entrance to the chamber. So the question is: can we conclude that the succession of arches was built outwards, away from the chamber, toward the roof-box, gradually reducing the light entering through it into the final, narrow beam?

I don't believe that we can, simply because the light-box itself is the smallest of the light-shaping arches. Therefore, the light beam had already been reduced to the precise dimensions required for the solstice observations. Remember, the roof-box was the first part of the structure to be completed. The chamber was the next item to be finalised.

(Unfortunately, both the standing stones that form the uprights of the arch at the entrance to the chamber had to be left as they were during the restoration, leaning inwards, thus reducing the size of the light beam to less than half its original size. In fact, Professor O'Kelly declined to straighten the inward-leaning standing stones lining the inner third of the passage because of the danger of collapse. Consequently, the size of the light beam is reduced even further. This deficiency was easily remedied in the scale model.)

So, the Solasídhe were quite satisfied with the dimensions of the light beam before they proceeded with the linking passage.

It follows logically that if the requirement was to observe the small differences in the position of the light between one sunrise and the next, then the dimensions of the beam of light had to remain the same from one sunrise to the next; it would make a nonsense of the observations if the light beam were to be reshaped by a second aperture. The effect on the light beam if it had to pass through a second aperture would be to reduce the number of observable alignments to one, and no one can glean much information from just one sunrise. Furthermore, the only way to tell that it was the all-important solstice sunrise, in that situation, would be by the brightness of the light, which would be a very imprecise and subjective measurement, to say the least.

Therefore, the two ranks of standing stones which form the passage were carefully placed, not only to avoid intruding on the painstakingly shaped light beam, but also to allow the light beam a certain amount of latitude. It had to be allowed to swing further and further to the side and down – without touching the sides of the passage – for a number of days on either side of the solstice. In other words, any further interference with the light coming in through the roof-box would have been counterproductive.

This seems to throw everything into confusion. It was all working out just fine until that last piece of precision engineering entered the equation. So are we at a dead end?

Not by any means. It's all very simple – every little thing is a vital part of the master plan. But we still have a little way to go to find the answer – the secret that I believe the Solasídhe kept from the Celts and the Christians.

9

ON REFLECTION

By the time they came to build Newgrange, the Solasídhe had spent more than 1,000 years developing that type of structure. Like any good builder – and the Solasídhe were good builders – they had become expert at it.

That means that the Solasídhe 'quantity surveyor' would not have been ordering material that wasn't going to be needed. The Solasídhe Master Builder would have had the carpenters' and the masons' productivity at a very high level, and after many attempts, the Solasídhe surveyors and architects would have had the whole thing off by rote.

The builders of Newgrange would also appear to have been minimalists in the technological sense of reducing everything to its most efficient functionality. They don't seem to have done much second guessing. There were no trial-and-error socket excavations in evidence for any of the standing stones. They appear to have been right the first time, every time. Nor were there any unused slabs left lying around the site: they were very tidy. Perhaps we are witnessing an early expression of the craftsman's dictum 'measure twice, cut once'.

It wasn't just an idle experiment when the Solasídhe decided to go the extremely dangerous route of corbelling the roof. Nor was it mere accident when they put the apex of the corbelled roof exactly where it is. They knew precisely what they were doing.

What they had laboured so diligently, efficiently and with great precision to achieve was to have the shear-legs in situ, with its apex vertically over the path of the incoming light beam and the passage pointing downhill, ready for the midwinter dawn.

And it's that last, small and seemingly paradoxical fact that's the crux of the whole business, because I believe that the Solasídhe secret was that they suspended a mirror from the apex of the shear-legs.

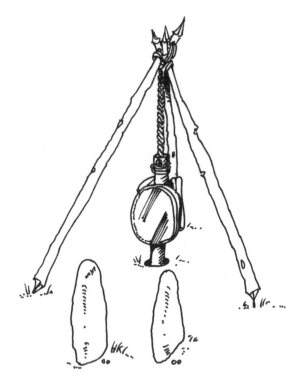

THE MIRROR

A very large mirror, or reflector, though I'm not yet certain what it was made of. What I *am* sure of is that using this large mirror, the Solasídhe reflected the incoming sunbeam back down the passage and out the front entrance.

When I replicated the situation with the scale model, using a theatre spotlight to represent the sun, I was astonished to find that the reflected beam was still clearly visible, as a sharply defined rectangle of light, at more than 45 metres' distance from the model. Forty-five metres in 1:24 scale is approximately equal to one kilometre in real time.

Perhaps it's all just coincidence, but at just about that distance away in real time, at the bottom of the valley, directly in line with the passage, is the Boyne River.

So what does it all mean?

It means that the connection between Newgrange and the Boyne is based in demonstrable fact, not just romantic legend or whimsical folklore. The connection between the river and the mound is real and is highly visible. Or to put it another way, if this connection in 1:24 scale can be replicated in full size, then the legends and the folklore have been telling the unvarnished truth.

The Solasídhe, with clear design intent, had con-structed this precision observatory in a slightly modified way, with the additional, simple but cunning objective of reflecting the golden light of midwinter sunrise down through the mist to strike the surface of the river.

And it certainly wasn't an afterthought or accident; there's no way that it was just a happy coincidence that became apparent after the structure had been completed. It was designed that way from the beginning, and the folklore of the pre-Celts preserved that knowledge down through all the millennia, down to our own time. But they never told the Celts or the Christians. Not the whole truth, anyway.

Whatever watered-down version of the truth the people did impart to the Celts resulted in the newcomers' Druids taking to lighting fires on the tops of the sacred hills,[1] which is a pale imitation of the real thing, given that the original was a kilometre-long shaft of reflected golden sunlight.

But that's not the whole story. There's quite a bit more to be revealed about the Solasídhe's solstice reflections.

First of all, the strange anomalies in the structure that I wondered about now begin to come clear. Of course they needed the curves in the passage down at the entrance. Of course they had to continue the passage on down the hill, because they were still shaping a light beam. But this time, the light was going the other way!

They obviously needed to have the apex of the corbelled chamber placed vertically over the path of the light if they were going to hang a reflector in the light. And of course they had to corbel the roof, because that's the only way they could accommodate the shear-legs.

It all makes logical sense.

It took me a long time to get the scale model to perform to the Solasídhe's specifications. The various elements could be clearly seen to be working, at different times. Getting all of the elements all working at the same time was the big problem.

Or so it seemed at the time.

You see, the model itself was working perfectly all the time, it's just that I didn't have any idea of what to expect. It was quite some time after I began the experiments that the truth began to dawn on me. I had started out with the notion that the reflected beam must have somehow dispersed, diffused or – more correctly – diffracted in the winter mist at the mouth of the passage. And so, I expected to see some sort of halo effect.

I spent many fruitless hours in various warehouses, attics and even outdoors in the winter dawn, trying to get the model to work. I used smoke machines, dry ice and cigarette smoke to try to reveal the light beam. I had used

spot lamps, flood lamps and all sorts of film-set techniques
to try and capture the reflected artificial sun, all to no avail.

It just never occurred to me that the light could possibly
have been reflected that huge distance. Consequently, all
my efforts had been concentrated far too close to the
model.

One of my original suppositions was that the mirror was
somehow formed with the famous basin stone. I even went
as far as getting real granite scale models made of it, with
various radii of curvature to try and make that work.

I eventually abandoned that line of enquiry when
Michael Heery, a man who knows even more about the
Solasídhe than I do, pointed out to me the obvious fact that
the focal length of such a mirror would be far too short to
reach the entrance to the passage.

Therefore, for the purposes of my experiments, I used a
small, flat, circular glass mirror. This little mirror was glued
to one arm of a small drawing compass. The compass, in
turn, was inverted and the apex mounted on a spindle. The
spindle was secured on a wooden mount in the base of the
model, below an aperture cut into the floor of the chamber.
Finally, the whole model was secured to the tilting table of
my studio drawing board.

By means of trial and error, tilting the table up and
down, I could usually succeed in getting the light to show
inside the model's chamber. Only when everything was set
up and locked off, with whatever light source I was using at
the time creating the primary shaft of incoming light,
could the mirror then be mounted on its spindle.

The whole arrangement succeeded in placing the little
round mirror directly in the path of the light. At the same
time, its angle to the light was controllable in both
horizontal and vertical axes.

The immensely delicate job of aiming the mirror would
then commence. By carefully rotating the screw-threaded
cross-bar on the drawing compass, the arms of the

instrument could be opened and closed, and so the attached mirror could be tilted forward and back.

And then, by simply rotating the whole mechanism on its vertical spindle, the mirror could be aimed at the very small target of the mouth of the passage.

As I have said before, even in this small scale, the clarity and sharpness of the light beam is quite startling, which is just as well, because there's no room for error at all. Any tiny deviation from the required direction immediately reduced the amount of light emanating from the model.

Manipulating such small and finicky mechanical devices inside a 1:24 scale model isn't the easiest task for human hands. The delicacy of adjustment required to make the model perform properly is quite demanding on the nerves. The tiniest of inadvertent movements of the mirror while locking it off is enough to upset the entire arrangement.

It was while engaged in this exercise for the umpteenth time that I realised that the front entrance must be closed in order to see the incoming light beam properly. Otherwise, the powerful spill of light through the entrance prevents it from being seen clearly.

But that wasn't the end of it. Having set up all the mechanical bits and pieces satisfactorily, it was now time to reveal the shaft of reflected light as it streamed out of the model.

In the real-time, original, full-scale operation, the light was directed down into the valley, which was filled with the mists of winter. The mist, hanging in the still air, created the perfect medium by which to reveal the light beam.

As well as that, the sunrise cast a deep shadow in the valley, as it still does, thus enhancing the whole effect. Recreating all those finely balanced factors in 1:24 scale is extremely difficult. The actual size of the site that would be required in order to see the 1:24 scale model working fully is about 150 metres long by 10 metres wide and five metres high, so as to get the river surface at about eye level. The whole area would have to be enclosed to keep the air still. Some means of introducing a water vapour, under very delicate control, would then have to be devised, and so on.

The only alternative would have been to build a full-scale model and wait until the solstice to make it work. That would mean either finding a replica of the original site, or recreating it, adjacent to a suitable river. I just had to work with the 1:24 scale model and compensate as I went along.

Finding a suitable light source was the first series of trials and errors. At the outset, I was inclined to use lamps that were too powerful, until I realised that the winter solstice sun is actually quite weak and watery in terms of luminosity – it's the golden colour of the light which is probably more important than the strength of it.

The situation in the Boyne Valley at midwinter dawn is a delicately balanced set of circumstances. The combination of weak but brilliantly golden sunlight rising at such an agonisingly slow and low trajectory creates enormously long and sharply defined shadows.

The valley remains in deep shadow long after the dazzling golden sunlight has illuminated the quartz facing of Newgrange. The valley is also filled with a thick mist from the river, hanging in the still air. Newgrange itself stands above the mist in the crisp, clear winter air.

The mist is one of the most vital elements in this scenario. It's the medium by which the golden shaft of light was revealed, streaking the one-kilometre distance down to the river's surface. Without the mist, it would be virtually impossible to see the shaft of light, except from a position directly in line with the passage, practically looking straight up at the mirror.

I have already stated that I don't know which material was used for the manufacture of the original mirror, but in all probability, it was gold. We know that some gold existed on the island in earliest times. In fact, recent discoveries reveal that there was – and still is – a great deal more gold in Ireland than was originally said to exist.

And, as we all know from the nineteenth-century gold rushes, gold is often found in nuggets, ready to hand, on the earth's surface.

You don't need to travel that far, either, as there was a gold rush of sorts in the same period in County Wicklow.

The Wicklow landscape is mostly bare, naked mountain, separated by lush, grassy glens, and it was the natural stronghold of the rebel Irish for many centuries. Consequently, knowledge of the discovery of gold was kept from the authorities for some time, possibly for a whole generation, before the secret leaked out and the government authorities moved in to take it over and extract what remained. To this day no one has any idea of the amount of gold that was extracted in the interim. What is known, however, is that the 'mother lode' was never found, so there's still a fortune in the precious metal to be uncovered in the Wicklow hills.

Gold, by its very nature, is easily worked. While it does require some heat to refine it from its ore, its melting point is even lower than that of copper. It's also relatively soft and malleable, instantly responsive to cold hammering.

Indeed, the early goldsmiths seem to have begun working the metal by doing just that – hammering it flat into extremely thin sheets. The technique then was probably the same as it is today – beating the gold flat between two sheets of tough horse-leather.

The inherent plasticity of the metal means that it can be worked and reworked in this manner without fracturing; quite a small amount can be beaten to such a thinness that it will cover a surprisingly large area. It has been claimed that a skilled artisan could take an ounce of the metal and beat a square yard of gold leaf from it.

Gold can also be burnished to a very high polish.

Modern goldsmiths use a substance called jeweller's rouge, derived from a stone called haematite, for this purpose. Haematite is so-called due to the fact that it's often stained red, as in the Greek root word for blood, and is actually one of the ores of iron, thus it's sometimes called ironstone.

If there's one subject on which late Stone Age civilisations could be expected to be expert it's stone. Even in much earlier times, different types of stone, such as flint, were being put to various uses consistent with their natural characteristics. And haematite is abundantly available in Ireland.

Maybe it's just another coincidence, but on p. 136 of Professor Michael Herity's book *Irish Passage Graves*, of which I possess a copy of the American edition, there's a splendid photographic reproduction[2] of a pair of apple-sized, polished stone balls. They had been discovered in the 'passage tombs' at Loughcrew, to the west of Newgrange. One of them is described as being made of ironstone.

Professor O'Kelly's wife, Claire, was adamant that none of the stones at Newgrange had ever been polished.[3] But *something* must have been polished, considering the number of stone and chalk balls and pieces of bone that had been found buried in the floor of the chamber, all of which had clearly been used for polishing and burnishing.

An important requirement when polishing a thin sheet of gold is a solid, flat surface. There are some very large, flat, round stones lying in the alcoves in the chamber in Newgrange. The faces of these stones, unique among all the stones in the building, appear to have been worked to a near-perfect flatness.

Presumably, the nearly flat surface of such stones could have been improved by the application of a slurry of softer material such as chalk or clay, perhaps dried over a fire, to smooth out bumps and hollows. A thin sheet of gold could then be laid on the filled surface of the flat stone, with the centre of the sheet kept in place with a thin film of animal grease or similar material, while the edge of the gold sheet was wrapped over the rim of the stone. The action of burnishing the gold sheet in situ would further improve the smoothness of the surface.

The resulting mirror could then be supported in some sort of cradle in order to suspend it from the shear-legs. The most efficient mechanical arrangement for such a cradle is as follows. Using the minimum amount of material, the construction is a skeletal pyramid of connected triangles, ensuring stability in all dimensions. The result is much like a cage, safely locking the heavy mirror within.

The whole apparatus was then hoisted up with the shear-legs, suspended by its apex from the main rope. The plane of the mirror's surface would then have required tilting to the correct angle of incidence.

By joining the rear-most point of the cradle, that is, the one at the back of the mirror, to the main suspension rope and then twisting the fibres of the secondary rope with a spike, thereby shortening it, the whole cradle was tilted.

This simple mechanical device, or Spanish windlass, as it's known in modern times, quickly brought the mirror's surface into the correct angle of incidence to reflect the incoming light; and since the whole apparatus was suspended, it was easily rotated into the required horizontal alignment so as to aim the reflected light with great accuracy out the entrance, just as easily as the vertical observation stone had been rotated when the site was being surveyed originally.

But before any light can enter the roof-box to begin the whole sequence, there was one very important little procedure to be carried out: taking the two white quartz closing stones out of the roof-box. The edges of the one that Professor O'Kelly discovered, in situ, had been worn smooth from repeated removals and replacements.[4]

With the stones once more removed, the Solasídhe technology sprang to life. The incredibly sharp shaft of light streaking in through the gloomy interior struck the surface of the mirror, reflecting itself back the way it had come.

Or, *almost* back the way it had come.

One important point to note about the mirror, now firmly caged in its cradle, is that it was suspended very low down, close to the floor. It's only in that position that it could intercept the incoming light beam.

More importantly, it's only in that one critical position where it can intercept the incoming light *and* reflect it back down the passage. The amazing precision with which the Solasídhe Master Observer surveyed the site only becomes apparent when you come to examine this critical positioning of the mirror. Absolutely no other position in the chamber or passage will meet the specifications.

The line of sight from the distant river through the entrance can only intersect the line of sight from the horizon through the roof-box at one point. That point is occupied by the centre of the mirror.

The Solasídhe Mirror Master had to work very quickly from behind the mirror, operating the Spanish windlass, tightening and shortening the rope, while at the same time observing the changing position of the rectangle of reflected light, aiming it at the target of the closing stone at the entrance.

I wonder if the Solasídhe had a target carved into the closing stone as a guide to the correct position. This stone, which now stands clamped to the wall outside the entrance, had lain flat on the ground in front of the entrance for many years. It had consequently been worn smooth by the feet of visitors as they entered and left the building. Any designs that might have existed on it would have been obliterated long ago.[5]

It had originally formed a snug-fitting 'front door' for the building, but it appears to have been in the open position, tilted back against the recumbent entrance stone, when the collapse of the building occurred in prehistory.

Incidentally, if it was still in position today and one were to push it outwards from inside the passage, it would rotate on its bottom edge,[6] much like a drawbridge, to lie up against the large recumbent stone outside the entrance to form a sloping ramp, just as it was originally designed to do.

Meanwhile, back in the chamber, the big mirror has successfully been hung in its cage, clear of the floor. There are many good reasons why the Solasídhe Mirror Master chose not to hang the mirror high up. If there was any mishap, for instance, it wouldn't fall too far and perhaps smash. There would also be less risk of injury – a very real danger in the confines of the chamber with a big mirror crashing down, out of control. It's also, of course, in a much more accessible position for the Mirror Master for the delicate work of alignment.

At a height of six metres and with a floor plan forming an equilateral triangle with sides of similar dimension, the shear-legs was quite capable of suspending a weight of some tonnes.

Just how massive the maximum size of the mirror stone could have been would have depended on the size of the timbers used in the construction. I think I have revealed enough of the Solasídhe building philosophy at this stage to be able to reasonably surmise that the timbers were probably quite massive.

But why didn't they simply prop the mirror up on the floor? Wouldn't that have avoided the need for all the contraptions, shear-legs, cradles and all? Even better, wouldn't it have done away with the need to corbel the roof in the first place?

The simple answer is that the sunrise is a complex dynamic process. As Newgrange spins around on the earth's slightly eccentric polar axis every day at close to 1,000 kilometres per hour, the whole globe itself is thundering along on its annual trip around the sun at over

100,000 kilometres per hour. Meanwhile, the sun, planets, moons and all are gently revolving with the rest of the Milky Way galaxy at speeds that I don't have room enough to write the zeros for. Trying to align a megalithic observatory with the one single sunrise that occurs exactly as the earth passes the halfway mark on its solar orbit is about the equivalent of trying to shoot clay pigeons while riding around and around on a merry-go-round.

Even when the Solasídhe succeeded in getting the alignment right, for how long did it stay that way?

Not very long.

The whole show at Newgrange, from beginning to end, lasts just 17 minutes.[7] The light beam keeps moving downwards and sideways as the sun rises at an angle. Therefore, to get the best value out of the situation, the obvious answer would be to keep the mirror moving in concert with the sunbeam.

One way to do that is to wind the whole mirror apparatus round and round on its main suspension rope. The more it's wound, the shorter the rope will become, exactly as for the Spanish windlass tilting mechanism.

When released, the mirror will begin to unwind under its own weight, keeping pace with the downward movement of the incoming sunbeam, turning slowly at first, then getting faster and faster, until it would fully unwind, whereupon it will try to wind itself up again under its own momentum.

Each time it passes through the full frontal position, it will flash the sunbeam down the valley to the waters of the Boyne, thereby creating the 'many chequered lights' with which we began this story.

At this point, I must update this text from the first edition for the sake of accuracy. In the first edition, the foregoing description of the mirror mechanism was based entirely on the scale model, in which the mirror mechanism was static for the very good reason that it was impossible to build a rotating version at that scale. In fact, for the purpose of experiment I did build a motorised version, with the works sitting on the baseboard and the axle coming up through floor of the chamber, rotating at close to 60 rpm. Ironically, that arrangement turns out to be closer to the real-time original than the static model that I described.

In truth, the static model turned out to be somewhat of a heresy; it seemed like a good idea at the time, and entirely plausible, but on reflection, this contraption, had it been installed and set in motion in real time, would not only have wrecked itself, killing the operators in the process, but could conceivably have demolished the entire corbelled chamber as well.

The whole mirror apparatus as described would weigh more than one tonne and would be fatally unstable when rotating at anything above 10 revolutions per minute (10 rpm); the optimum maximum speed of rotation for the proper effect would be more like 60 rpm, or one revolution per second.

At that rate of rotation, unless there was some form of restraining axle or socket below the apparatus, it would begin to react to any small imbalances in its structure and start to oscillate, spinning further and further out of alignment, until it would begin wildly bashing from one wall to the other, splintering the wooden cage, probably dislodging the feet of the shear-legs, thereby releasing the rapidly spinning mirror stone to smash the standing stones out of their sockets, destroying the structural integrity of the corbelled roof, which would instantly collapse, finally pulverising the renegade mirror into submission. Rotating machinery is very, very dangerous.

So I revisited the mirror mechanism and redesigned it, bearing in mind the deficiencies of the prototype. What emerged was a much more stable and safe mechanism, consisting of a main axle, a sturdy, straight pole about three metres in length, which would be suspended by one end from the main rope hanging from the apex of the shear-legs, just like the errant prototype.

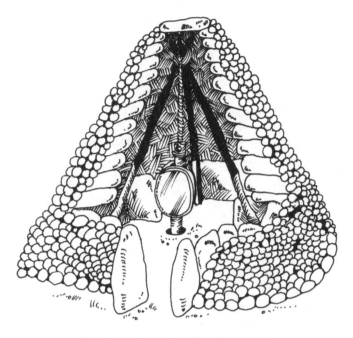

THE MIRROR MECHANISM

Strapped to the pole would be three mirror stones, back to back, with a Spanish windlass tilting mechanism incorporated for each mirror, but each of these of much smaller dimensions than the prototype.

The other end of the pole would be inserted in a close-fitting pit in the centre of the chamber floor. This pit would be deep enough to accommodate the descent of the main pole as it unwound itself from the pre-twisted main suspension rope, and would probably be lubricated with animal fat to smooth the operation. It might even be lined with small rounded pebbles to minimise the friction.

In other words, the pit would act as a stabilising and retaining bearing for the main axle of the mechanism, creating a much neater, safer and more efficient arrangement altogether.

Naturally, you might ask if there's any evidence to support this revised design of the mirror mechanism. In Professor O'Kelly's report, he states: 'Another smaller pit was found in the central chamber and this appeared to have been dug from the old floor level. It was about 150 cm deep, filled with broken stones in dark earth. The mixture had the appearance of being deliberately buried. The pit does not seem to have been original nor even very ancient.'[8]

However, earlier on the same page, Professor O'Kelly refers to the great amount of disturbance to the floor of the chamber in 'relatively recent' times and 'some of it a good deal further back in time'. The inference appears to be that treasure hunters and the like had been digging pits all over the place, and that our little pit was just another one of these; whatever the reason, no further investigation of the pit appears to have been undertaken, which means the possibility of firm corroborating evidence for the improved mirror mechanism has been lost forever. Perhaps another, so far unexcavated mound will provide the answer in the future.

So, based on the facts so far and the coincidental fragments of other evidence, if you were to reassemble the Solasídhe reflecting technology for the next winter solstice at Newgrange – and it could be done – what would the effect be? What would anybody see?

I believe that you would see a recreation of the world's very first outdoor drama, a Neolithic 'mega-happening', the scale of which would blow the minds of some of our modern rock concert buffs. So what did it do to the minds of the audience gathered on the terraces on the far side of the river 5,000 years ago?

You could say that it affected them to the extent that,

among other things, their oral tradition preserved the knowledge in strange-seeming stories, through five millennia, down to the present day. But in all that time, the descendants of those who witnessed the Solasídhe dominance over the sun refused to tell any of the successive waves of invading strangers the full story: 'I won't tell you everything I know, because you would then be wiser than I am myself.'

10

THE AMPHITHEATRE

It's getting close to the time for examining the external clues to the Solasídhe's secret of Newgrange. The show is about to start, but you must understand the gigantic scale of what you are about to witness; it is time to take you on a tour of the most amazing outdoor theatre in history. Only then will you appreciate the failure of modern technology to improve on the prehistoric original.

If we had emerged from the passage at Newgrange and walked up the ramp formed by the closing stone to stand on top of the huge 'decorated' stone outside the entrance and looked down into the Boyne Valley, what would we have seen? We would have seen a typical Irish rural farmland scene, with glimpses of the distant Boyne River in the gaps between the field hedges, sweeping through the valley.

But if we were to survey the scene through the eyes of the Solasídhe Master Builder, what would be different?

For one thing, there would be many more trees, except on the hill directly below us; it was cleared of trees. In fact, even the green turf had been stripped off the side of the hill.[1] There would be few farmhouses, and even fewer hedges.

The steep slope of the terracing on the far bank would look much as it does today. It seems to form terracing as it rises to the horizon. It is actually called glacial terracing by geologists, as it was formed by the glacier that gouged out the valley not too long before Newgrange was built.

The natural terracing stretches for roughly three to four kilometres and forms a near-perfect semi-circle. A very large semi-circle. So large, in fact, that it may not be readily apparent as such to us as casual observers. But the Solasídhe Master Builder was anything but a casual observer.

It will become abundantly clear that the size and shape of the Boyne Valley itself was what decided the Solasídhe on their grand master plan. Because just exactly where we would be standing is the geometrically exact focal point of that huge semi-circle.

There's only one other writer, to my knowledge, who has commented on the fact that on the south bank of the Boyne, on the far side of the river from Newgrange, the ground rises in natural glacial terracing to a height of 30 metres. The same writer remarks how the Boyne River describes an almost perfect semi-circle around the foot of the hill, with Newgrange as a focal point at its centre: The whole constituted a superb natural amphitheatre.'[2]

Quite so. I believe that Newgrange is actually sited centre-stage in the largest natural amphitheatre in the world, and I also believe that the Solasídhe Master Builder chose the site for that very reason.

I have satisfactorily demonstrated that the Solasídhe were technological minimalists, that they were superb planners and that they didn't do things idly or by accident.

Four kilometres of terracing, 30 metres high, will comfortably accommodate 250,000 seated people. The Solasídhe weren't short of sites. There's an abundance of other sites where the same thing could have been done on a much smaller scale. The Boyne Valley isn't the only meandering river valley on the island. They chose this one very carefully.

Which, if true, raises a number of questions. Did they have a 'full house' audience on the terracing? If so, where did they all come from? Did they come back every year, or just once in a lifetime? But most importantly, what were they doing there? What did they expect to see?

There are those[3] who disagree with the style of Professor O'Kelly's reconstruction of Newgrange, and I have to admit that I'm one of them. Undoubtedly, a start had to be made somewhere, and an end to the work at Newgrange certainly had to be declared sometime. Otherwise, archaeological teams could still be delving into the mysteries of the site. My own feeling is that the completion of the work at Newgrange was not an end, but a beginning.

My bible of reference for my work was, and still is, Professor O'Kelly's excavation report. I have been criticised for not drawing on a wider spectrum of scholarship on other Neolithic structures and for failing to cross-reference the various features which are common to many of the structures of the period. I confess to being unrepentant on both counts. I am unrepentant because Newgrange is unique and will, I believe, remain so. There has been some weak speculation that other structures could/might/should contain 'roof-boxes' or equivalents. Nothing more has been heard.

Perhaps the focus on comparisons is misplaced. No doubt other structures were designed to perform light effects, but not on the scale or complexity of that performed at Newgrange. In my view, Newgrange represents the culmination of Neolithic technology. I also believe that the technology was superseded in a quantum leap equivalent in effect to the invention of the transistor or the computer, which is why there was no attempt made in prehistory to restore Newgrange – because it had become redundant, obsolete.

But the restored structure is, I feel, somewhat incongruous. It appears to me to be in some way awkward; it seems uncomfortably contrived. As a designer, I find that it fails to dominate the site as it should, that it lacks harmony with its situation.

Even though Professor O'Kelly realised that Newgrange was sited in a particularly commanding situation, especially when viewed from the other side of the Boyne River, he was apparently not able to capitalise on the fact.

The sorry state of the collapsed structure of Newgrange prior to its restoration from 1963 to 1975 gave rise to many speculations as to its original size and shape. Professor O'Kelly himself was quite adamant that his restoration faithfully replicated the original, except for the necessary minor changes to the entrance area. He naturally based this view on his own interpretation of the evidence of its collapse, as he found it.

Other commentators have maintained (without offering much in the way of supporting evidence) that the structure must have been much higher, in one case as much as 30 metres higher.[4] Based on his own firm conclusions, Professor O'Kelly tends to display some impatience, not to say irritation, with these theories.

Correspondingly variable estimates have been made of the amount of material remaining in the structure, again without convincing evidence being presented: Professor O'Kelly calculated 200,000 tonnes; Mitchell, before him, indicated just 50,000.[5] I believe I may be able to give some help towards the settlement of the arguments.

Professor O'Kelly appeared to prove to everyone's satisfaction that the proposed 'near vertical wall of white quartz' surrounding the drum-shaped mound had fallen 'in a fairly rapid and clean collapse...due to the outward movement of the kerbstones as settlement pressures developed behind them.'[6] His clever reconstruction and deliberate destruction of a short section of this '*projet* perimeter', which supposedly replicated the original fall of material, seemed conclusive.[7]

His theory begins with the supposition that the kerbstones had fallen outwards under the influence of 'internal settlement pressures'. What concerns me is the amount of pressure that would have been required to cause most of the kerbstones to lean outwards, all at the same time. They had all been set into shallow sockets and propped in place with smaller stones, and none of them weigh less than one tonne.

If the proposed revetment wall had been built on the top of the kerb, as envisaged by Professor O'Kelly, it seems to me that it would have served to add to the stability of the kerb. If internal settlement pressures had developed, surely it would only have been the revetment wall itself which would have collapsed outwards, without disturbing the kerbstones.

Thus, I have grave difficulty with Professor O'Kelly's seemingly well-reasoned and ably demonstrated theory that the reconstructed white quartz wall replicates the original. Nor do I believe that the original collapsed in exactly the manner he demonstrated.

And therein lies a paradox, because I also believe that he was absolutely correct on both counts. I do believe that his reconstructed revetment wall does faithfully replicate the original – but only for the last two or three seconds of its original existence.

In his fascinating book *The Riddle of the Pyramids*,[8] the Egyptologist Professor Kurt Mendelssohn literally turned the established view of the sequence in which the Egyptian pyramids had been built upside down. It had long been held by the experts as indisputable fact that as the Egyptian economy began to collapse, the second last pyramid, that of Snofru, the so-called 'Bent' Pyramid at Dashur, was already half completed, and so it was quickly finished at a much shallower angle.

It was also Egyptological gospel that the very last of the pyramids, that of Meidum, 45 kilometres to the south of Dashur, never got beyond the first stages of construction. Its internal skeletal buttress walls – its foundations, so to speak – stand in a mound of debris, believed by all to have been created by the removal of large quantities of stone from the uncompleted structure.

However, with the aid of aerial photography, Mendelssohn showed that in fact the Meidum pyramid, the so-called 'Last Pyramid', was actually the *first* in the series to be built. It had in fact been fully completed and clad in a smooth mantle of dressed limestone, but had then collapsed catastrophically. Mendelssohn also showed that the collapse had been caused by using badly squared blocks of soft limestone in the construction, and not by the actions of stone robbers.

He went on to show that the Bent Pyramid at Dashur had been half completed at an angle of 52.5°, the same steep angle as the doomed prototype, when the catastrophe occurred at Meidum.

Surmising that the architects must have realised that they were building the pyramids too steeply for stability given the inferior quality of masonry, Mendelssohn concluded that they finished off the pyramid of Dashur at the safer, lower angle of 43.5°, bestowing on the structure its distinctive 'bent' shape.

He extended his theory by pointing out that because the Red Pyramid, also at Dashur, was also built at this safe lower angle, it must have been the next pyramid to be built.

However, all the later pyramids reverted to the steeper angle of 52.5°. According to Mendelssohn, this was because of the lesson learned from Meidum, since all the later, steeper pyramids are built of very well-squared blocks.

He went further. Using a modelling clay mock-up, he demonstrated what happens to unbonded structures composed of unstable materials, such as unsquared blocks or rough masonry, when they're piled up too steeply. Under the influence of their own weight, they will develop 'plastic flow', which essentially means that they will behave like a super-thick liquid and flow to the lowest level.

Newgrange was originally composed for the most part of unbonded water-rolled pebbles, which means that it was extremely unstable. It also means that if it were to be piled up high enough, plastic flow would inevitably develop, just as the Egyptians were to discover some centuries later, to their cost.

There are two significant differences between Newgrange and the pyramids. Firstly, Newgrange is built at the top of a hill, and secondly, it's bounded by an enclosing kerb of very large boulders set up on their lengthwise edges. When Professor O'Kelly unearthed them, most of them had toppled outwards, lying flat on their backs.

On the outside of them, lying on the original surface of the hill, he found a carpet of white quartz pieces, which he correctly surmised was the original outer covering of the building. It was this discovery that led the professor to the conclusion that the fallen quartz pieces had formed a revetment, or near vertical, wall standing on top of the now-toppled stones. This seemed like a reasonable idea at the time.

He further supported his theory that the building had originally been bounded by this near-vertical revetment or wall of white quartz by the brilliantly simple expedient of rebuilding a short section of the supposed wall on top of the replaced boulders, and then deliberately causing it to collapse. Not surprisingly, the artificial results replicated the original findings almost exactly. Happy with his ingenuity, Professor O'Kelly gathered up the remaining material and proceeded to restore the structure to its present drum-shaped condition, which, on the face of it, also seemed entirely reasonable, except that, as he tells us himself, he discounted as being unreliable all the reports – particularly those of Pownall, an eighteenth-century writer who is the chief source for all subsequent writers on Newgrange – which tell us that 'all the roads in the neighbourhood are paved with its [Newgrange's] stones; immense quantities have been taken away'.[9]

What if, like so many other strange stories, they were all in fact true? Wouldn't it mean that the original structure was larger than it is today? If it were larger, and yet the bounding kerb of boulders has been restored to its original position, wouldn't it therefore mean that the structure must have been higher? And if it was higher, it can hardly have been drum shaped, certainly not with a perimeter wall as steep as that proposed.

Since Professor O'Kelly's theory countenanced a collapse at a much lower height, it can be reasonably supposed that a similar but higher rubble wall of unbonded stones could not have sustained itself long enough for it to have been completed.

Following Mendelssohn's plastic flow theory for a moment, let's suppose, for the purpose of the argument, that the structure was considerably higher. Not drum shaped, but more in the form of a shallow cone, high enough, and steep enough, and built of such inherently unstable material that its own internal forces, instead of being directed vertically downwards, were instead deflected sideways. These forces would have caused the retaining kerb of boulders to be put under pressure. The whole structure would have been held in equilibrium by the stabilising mass of the kerb of boulders holding the internal pressures at bay.

This delicate state of equilibrium would have continued until some other force, perhaps an earth tremor,[10] would have unlocked the inherent instability, causing the kerb of boulders to be displaced by the pent-up internal forces. Most of them would then have capsized outwards, destroying the equilibrium of the whole pile. Plastic flow would then have commenced.

The whole artificial mountain of material would have subsided in the centre, bulging upwards and outwards around the rim, apparently in slow motion, causing the white quartz covering to rise up and stand almost vertically, poised for one awful moment in time, before spilling

109

outwards over the capsized kerbstones to fall as a carpet on the downhill side of the displaced kerb. The rest of the material would have then flowed, unrestrained, out over the sloping ramp formed by the first material, gathering speed on its way off down the hill, a thunderous avalanche of hundreds of thousands of tonnes of small boulders and quartz pieces mixed with earth, sweeping all before it, ripping most of the outer circle of standing stones out of their sockets, snapping others off at ground level, to join the tidal wave of destruction sweeping down the hill to come to rest in the fold of the terraced fields below.

When the dust finally settled, what would have remained for future investigators is exactly what Professor O'Kelly found, including evidence of secondary, minor avalanches and rockslides which continued intermittently as the ruined structure was further eroded by the elements.

The persistent local reports over the years of much white quartz being turned up by ploughing activity down in the terraced fields, and other reports claiming that the origin of the quartz lies on the bed of the Boyne River, gives me some hope that a few exploratory trenches, properly licensed and professionally supervised, could turn up something of interest.

So just exactly how high would the monument have had to have been to cause itself to collapse?

There are two ways to approach that question. Firstly, I'm sure engineers would be able to work it out with a few formulae and some calculations, but I'd like to try it from a slightly different direction, where the answer to that question depends on the answers to one or two others.

You'll have noticed that everyone seems to be agreed on a white quartz covering on the structure, when actually it was only faced with quartz on the south side. Professor O'Kelly found absolutely no evidence of any quartz on the north side. There must have been a good reason for that. The reason is, of course, the sun.

Don't forget that this is essentially a solar structure; the whole purpose for building it in the first place was to observe the sun. When the sun would rise, particularly around the time of the solstice, it would make the whole south-east face of the structure glow in a sparkling, golden light, reflecting the sunrise from the quartz.

Even today, that would still be quite a spectacular show.

But there wouldn't have been much point in covering the north side of the building in quartz, firstly because the sun wouldn't reach it, and secondly, there would have been nobody around the back to see it anyway, because they would have all been on the terraces, on the south side of the Boyne.

Newgrange is at an elevation of 60 metres. The horizon to the south-east, behind and beyond the glacial terracing, is at 120 metres. When the solstice sun peeps over that horizon these days, it's lighting the empty sky above Newgrange for some time before it rises high enough for its rays to strike the present quartz wall.

In fact, its light doesn't penetrate the roof-box until the full disc of the sun is clear of the horizon. It never did otherwise, because it's important for the solstice observations that the full diameter of the sun passes in front of the roof-box aperture.

Now, if the plan with the quartz light show was to impress the people gathered on the far terracing, would the Master Builder really have missed the golden opportunity of lighting the building from the earliest possible moment? After all the trouble they had already gone to, I believe that it's a reasonable proposition that they did heap up the structure to a height of perhaps 30 or so metres at the centre in order for the very first rays of the solstice sun to catch the very tip of the building, which was probably covered in white quartz all the way to the top. Wouldn't that make a much more impressive sight, totally dominating the site, visible for miles around, definitely a show that people would come to see?

The average diameter of the building is about 90 metres, so heaping it up to 30 metres at the centre would not have presented any great difficulty. Those dimensions would create a not very steep-sided structure, rather a very shallow one of 30°, which is much less steep than the Meidum Pyramid that was to collapse 500 years later and not even as steep as the later, 'safer' Red Pyramid at Dashur.

But it was much less stable than any of the pyramids, so unstable that it eventually collapsed in plastic flow under the influence of its own weight, even though it was built at a much lower angle. I say 'eventually', because Newgrange must have been in use for some time before it did fall down, simply because of the great wealth of folklore and legend that had time to become associated with it.

Was this what it was all about? Was the whole thing carefully contrived, using the natural topography of the situation? Was the whole thing deliberately designed to impress the people on the terraces with a pretty light show? If that was the case, what happened next? Don't forget that the primary purpose was to calibrate the passing of the solstice inside, in the chamber.

So, did the Master Observer then trudge the kilometre down the hill to the water's edge, when the chequered lights had faded, and announce to the multitudes on the terraces that all was well, that the year had turned? For the purpose of this story, let's suppose that that's exactly how it happened. But why would such an announcement have required such a vast arena? Would such a simple, un-dramatic – indeed, sober – presentation have attracted a vast number of people to hear it?

No. There was much, much more to the story.

You didn't suppose that the Master Observer was going to tell the whole story, did you, and thereby abandon the old proverb 'I won't tell you all that I know, because than you'd be as wise as I am myself'?

11

SON ET LUMIÈRE

Professor O'Kelly freely acknowledged that Newgrange was more impressive when viewed from the far side of the river, which isn't surprising when you understand what the object of the exercise was from the very beginning.

The Solasídhe had gone to all the elaborate and labour-intensive trouble of erecting the most technologically advanced, high-precision light-bending machine in the Neolithic world, carefully siting it at the focal point of the largest, most majestic natural amphitheatre they could find.

For what? So they could reflect a beam of light for 15 minutes once a year? That would hardly qualify it for prominence in the folklore as a myth-making, historic event.

The Solasídhe surely didn't rely solely on the visual impact of the building and its light show to impress their audience. You would naturally expect that they must have embellished and dramatised the event with supportive pomp and spectacle. They must surely have promoted and propagandised the event as well if they hoped to fill the terraces with an appreciative audience.

After all, the Solasídhe had the knowledge and owned the technology, so why wouldn't they want to flaunt it? Human nature doesn't change.

That someone could control the sun, causing it to appear to rise in the west, would certainly be an amazing thing to behold, but it was at best a once-a-year show. It was important that as many people as possible could view the phenomenon. But it was also important that the masses on the terraces should never tumble to the limitations inherent in the technology. There would have been no future for the Solasídhe if the mechanics of their little scheme had leaked out. Security, then as now, would have been paramount.

So how did they preserve and protect their vulnerable technology for so long?

I have already remarked on the fact that the Solasídhe appear to have been a peace-loving people, that there were no defences built around Newgrange. Or were there? The Boyne River is a defence. Its tributary, the Mattock, is also a defence. Natural defences.

It could well be that the Solasídhe didn't need to build artificial protection. Even today, and even after it has been canalised, the Boyne is still a formidable barrier. It forms an effective security barrier for the modern rock concerts that are held in the grounds of Slane Castle, just upriver from Newgrange, in the summertime. The Mattock, although a smaller river, would also have been a distinct deterrent, especially in winter.

Newgrange is sited on what amounts to a peninsula between the two rivers. It's actually very easily defended, without it appearing to be so. Could it be that the Solasídhe, who were obviously good psychologists, merely reinforced the public's reverence for this sacred place by not making it too easy to approach, except from the front?

The Boyne was probably navigable as far upriver as Newgrange and beyond in Neolithic times. The large low-lying floodplain below the structure was possibly created as a result of it being the limit of the tidal effect. Or did the tide affect the river level up as far as the natural weir at

Slane? Could it have been that the solstice audience, or at least some of them, arrived by boat? And if so, from where? If the size of the amphitheatre is any measure of the size of the audience, there could well have been many thousands of pilgrims who arrived by boat. And if there was any great amount of river traffic up as far as this, there would inevitably have to have been some prepared landing places. That is, if the boats were any larger than canoes.[1] If they were sailing craft, or multi-oared sea-going craft, for instance, they would have been too heavy to beach on the bank-side. They would have had to tie up at a quay. And that quay would most likely have been on the south bank. It would also have to have been either upstream or downstream from the amphitheatre. After all, the audience wouldn't have accepted their view being obstructed with a forest of ships' rigging.

The availability of berthage would have constituted one more factor in favour of the choice of this site. The Solasídhe would have grasped any opportunity for the furtherance of their technological dominance over the common people, particularly if there had been an international dimension to the scheme.

If there was a large amount of river traffic for any length of time, there would inevitably have been casualties over the years. It may well have been that the pilgrims continued to arrive throughout the remainder of the year, not just in time for the solstice.

All the hazards that attend water-borne transport at any time would have manifested themselves – collisions would have occurred, storm-damaged boats would have sunk, others would have foundered on uncharted rocks. As well as that, the usual detritus of cannibalised and abandoned hulls would have accumulated in the backwaters, just as they do today.

I wonder how much evidence would remain of such small disasters, preserved in the mud and silt of the original river course. The present-day channel does not necessarily follow the original. Hopefully, one day, properly conducted excavations in the adjacent environs of the Boyne will deliver up some clues to the standard of Neolithic marine architecture.

It's more than likely that the Solasídhe employed the same ingenuity and careful planning for the whole site in preparation for the annual solstice extravaganza as they had in building Newgrange itself. The size of the surrounding amphitheatre is vast in modern terms, but why not? The whole concept is vast, from start to finish.

At the bottom of the hill below Newgrange is a flat floodplain. There are traces of other structures there, including some small mounds and circular banks. But was it always that way? I suspect that at one time it was a carefully maintained flood meadow. It was most likely to have been controlled by Solasídhe weirs, cutting it off from the main current of the river. The resultant lake, or still pool of water, would have reflected a mirror image of everything on the slope above it.

It was on that still pool that the reflected beam of light would have impinged. Martin Brennan may have been closer to the truth than he thought when he wrote: 'The passageway at Newgrange would function as a sighting tube with which it would be possible not only to observe sun spots but also to see stars in broad daylight. By using a reflecting pool of water and a correctly aligned sighting tube, one can determine the moment of a star's transit to a split second.'[2]

So what form would a Solasídhe dramatisation of the event have taken? It's clear that the public event would have been an essentially outdoor performance. Whatever form the Solasídhe's astronomical calibrations took, they were essentially an indoor, therefore non-public, operation. The real reason for building the solstice observatory was known only to the chosen Solasídhe few who were qualified to peruse the interior calibrations. This astronomical elite would probably have considered the exterior, public light show to be very much secondary to the important work of solstice observation.

Only when their indoor work had been satisfactorily concluded would it have been time to inspire the masses. The priority, however, would always have been to complete the solstice observations satisfactorily. The whole purpose of the exercise was to discern with certainty the fact that the year had turned. Once that knowledge was safely within the Solasídhe remit, they could relax and prepare for the annual light show.

In all probability, the light show was managed by a totally separate crew. Or, more properly, a totally separate cast, because that's what the light show would have become – a theatrical performance.

There was probably a Solasídhe Master of Ceremonies, who would have directed the light show. Perhaps the Solasídhe played the light show as often as they could manage it, maybe even every morning of the entire fortnight. But somehow, I'm more inclined to think they operated on the old Irish proverbial principle that what's seldom is wonderful.

Besides, the Solasídhe astronomers had a priority requirement to observe a number of dawns on either side of the solstice before they could be sure of their facts, which would have reduced the number of possible days on which the show could be performed.

Meanwhile, let me paint you a picture: the pilgrim masses would probably have been gathering on the terraces, in high anticipation, for weeks beforehand. They would have mingled, exchanging news and gossip with friends and relations. Liaisons would have been conceived between nationalities. They would probably have traded food, furs and wood and bone ornaments, household implements and tools. It would have been like a fortnight of fair days.

Looking at the situation as the Solasídhe Master of Ceremonies might see it, there are immense possibilities, many wonderful ingredients that could be exploited in creating a stunningly memorable show.

The first question an MC would ask is: what would the audience see, standing here on the terraces of the Grand Circle on this side of the Boyne, if they looked up at Newgrange? At solstice time, of course, the whole valley, this huge amphitheatre, would be filled with a mixture of smoke from the campfires and mist from the river hanging in the deathly midwinter stillness. The whole effect, with the reflected beam of light shining down into the valley, would be something similar to the beam of a cinema projector hanging in dust and cigarette smoke, before the anti-smoking laws.

Or could it be that there was a ban on lighting fires because it might interfere with the visibility of the light show? Could it be that that's the origin of the much later Celtic edict, the one allegedly breached by St Patrick, forbidding the lighting of fires until the High King had lit the first one on the Hill of Tara? (Incidentally, Tara is visible from Newgrange, just 16 kilometres (10 miles) away to the south-west.)

Looking back up the hill toward the source of the light, the pilgrims would have seen Newgrange looming above the mist, brightly lit in the golden glow of the winter solstice dawn. The horizon would have been lost in the mist. The covering of white quartz would have been truly dazzling. The visual effect caused by gazing upwards, focusing on a bright object which possesses no apparent horizon, can be quite dramatic.

The effect would be to apparently magnify the bright object to cause it to appear to fill the field of vision. In this situation, it would also serve to exaggerate the strength of the beam of light. It would appear to be quite dazzling, too, as it struck the surface of the still-water pool.

But that's not all.

The Boyne is a salmon river. There's a body of Irish folklore and legend which centres on the salmon of the Boyne. Fionn MacCumhail, a legendary hero, was alleged to have burned his thumb on the hot flesh of a Boyne salmon. It was the Salmon of Knowledge that he had caught and cooked. Sticking his thumb in his mouth to cool it, Fionn discovered that all knowledge was revealed to him. Thereafter, when he wanted to know something, all he had to do was chew his thumb.

A similar legend is enshrined in Wagner's operas, based on German folklore, where the hero, Siegfried, sucks his thumb to similar effect.

The Boyne salmon were on their spawning run up-river around the time of the solstice, just as they do today. In Neolithic times, the number of salmon was vast, and the size of the individual fish was awe-inspiring – 20-, 30- and even 40-kilo fish would have been quite common.

All of these mouth-watering ingredients were already in place around solstice time. The job to be done by an MC would have been to dress up the show, using these ingredients to support and expand it all into one huge, spectacular, memorable, magic performance.

The second thing the MC would have done was to meet the Music Master.

There's no doubt in my mind that the Solasídhe used music to augment the light show. I'm also sure that the musical technology available would have been fairly basic – a choir of voices, some percussion and maybe simple woodwind instruments. But there's no doubt that they would have applied the same principles of scale to the musical arrangements as they had for everything else.

The key to the whole show, of course, was to demonstrate that the Solasídhe were in command of the sun. Therefore, any such demonstration would have required close co-operation between the mechanical and musical elements.

There would have been no gain in having the choir and orchestra out of synchronisation with the chequered lights, so it follows logically that the Music Master and the Mirror Master often rehearsed their people together.

I surmise that the MC arranged the musicians at the bottom of the slope, below Newgrange, where there's a bank of glacial terracing on the north bank of the river, directly facing the centre of the amphitheatre, directly above the still-pool. The choir and orchestra, ranged on this terracing, are much closer to the audience, and their combined musical output is perfectly positioned for maximum volume.

The slope is stripped bare of turf, with the exposed shale blackly gleaming. The three ranks of woodwinds are lowest on the hill, with their alpine horn-type instruments resting on the slope below them, almost in the water.

The drums take station uphill of the woodwinds, and the choir are massed further uphill again, almost at the top of the bank.

The orchestra would probably have made a ceremonial entrance in the pre-dawn light and taken their places, all dressed in white. Most likely, the members of the orchestra would have entered on the scene from behind the mound of Newgrange, followed by the choir parading down the slope to take their positions. Their appearance was probably designed to silence the audience in expectation.

As the solstice sun peeps over the Red Mountain to the south-east, the choir, as cue leaders, begin a slow chant; the orchestra follows.

A slow, sustained rhythm on the drums is supported by the sonorous *basso continuo* of the woodwinds. Four minutes later, the sun enters the roof-box.

The next cue is in the Mirror Master's hands. The mirror crew would have had to work very quickly to orientate the mirror. As soon as they were ready, they would have covered the mirror with a quickly removable cover. The cue for the choir is the closing stone being

120

levered open by the mirror crew, signalling that everything is set up, ready to go. As the door-opening crew dash back up the passage to operate the mirror, it's SHOWTIME!

The massed voices swell in volume, pitching higher and higher. As they reach the limit of their power, they climax in an ear-piercing shriek – the cue for the mirror crew to whip the mirror covering aside.

The first shaft of light streaks down into the valley, seemingly at the command of the Solasídhe choir. But inside, the mirror has started turning. The light slowly fades. The choir begins again, swelling and rising until their climactic shriek coincides, each time, with the reappearance of the light.

The percussion rhythm gradually begins to speed up the tempo, matching the accelerating frequency of light flashes, all the time supported by the deep rumble of the bass woodwinds. Soon, the cadence of the light's flashing and choir's shrieking matches the pounding of the heart's pulse.

At the climax of this sound and fury, the Solasídhe Weir Master releases the pent-up shoals of salmon. Their only path to their goal of the spawning beds is through the shallow still-pool.

Cleverly hidden just below the surface, the Weir Master has built low barriers, a series of mini stone walls. The magnificent silver fish thrash their way through the shallows, leaping out of the water to clear the hidden walls.

And all the time, the light continues to flash down on the pool. The thrashing fish beat the water to a foam in their furious drive onward, breaking the light into sparkles and rainbows.

The crowds on the terraces ooh and aah in delight and wonder.

Then everything begins to fade.

The rhythm of sound and light gradually slows and stops. As the last weak flash of light slowly fades, the last of the salmon gains the deeper water upstream.

All becomes quiet.

The white-robed choir proceeds majestically, slowly, back up the slope, their flowing garments shimmering in the morning sunlight as they disappear around each side of Newgrange, all to the thunderous applause of the audience on the terraces.

The Master of Ceremonies then announces in a loud voice that the year has turned, the Sun God is in his heaven, and everyone is safe for another year.

Although Newgrange's roof-box is, so far, unique, there's ample evidence that many other similar structures contain the corbelled accommodation for a shear-legs. Newgrange probably represents the zenith of the Solasídhe technology, but as they progressed with the development of their technology, it remains to be discovered just exactly where it all began. And where it all ended.

I find it hard to accept that the whole magnificent culture just suddenly 'upped stakes' and disappeared. They must have progressed with the chequered lights technology some-where. Perhaps it blossomed into a totally different form, unrecognisable to eyes searching for megalithic evidence?

But on the way, the development of the known tech-niques could very well have resulted in the dimensions of the mechanical items becoming standardised, for instance. There would have been obvious advantage in having all mirrors rotate at a consistent rate from one structure to the next: there would have been only one tune to be learned.

And how could a simple, peasant people explain all of that to the strangers? They could only have told them what they understood, and then not all of that. They would never have told the strangers the full story, anyway.

But I have told you everything I know, so you are now as wise as I am myself.

EPILOGUE

Well, I have told you everything I knew up to the middle of 2004, but there's one new piece of information that I would like you to have: I was walking the floodplain field below Newgrange in the company of a colleague, Kieran Comerford, an engineer who has a great interest in Newgrange from the perspective of energy fields, and who had accompanied me on one of my excursions to the locality to test one of his ideas by dowsing, or divining, with metal rods.

Now, I am no expert by any means in divining, but I have dabbled in it. Having helped him to find the energy fields he was looking for, we turned to head for home. Absolutely impromptu, I suggested that we do a quick divining for the low walls that I had predicted in the final chapter of the book – the walls under the surface of the still pool that the salmon were made to leap over.

He chuckled good-naturedly, not being a convinced adherent to my theory, but readily agreed. So we set off, parallel with the river, about 10 metres apart. Within a few paces both sets of divining rods signalled strongly and simultaneously. I shrugged, dismissing it as probably a drain or such, and we proceeded. At exactly 10 paces further on, the rods signalled again, simultaneously, and just as strongly. At every 10 pace interval, the rods signalled strongly and simultaneously for the next 100 metres or so.

We had to call a halt at that because we were running short of time for an appointment back in Dublin. We were silent on the drive back, fairly well gobsmacked at our experience. Later in the week, having considered the experience at some length, I decided to seek an independent review by an experienced diviner.

Who better than the charming Moya Henderson, Secretary of the Irish Diviner's Society, who readily agreed to meet at the site the following week. With no prior clue as to what she was expected to find, Moya straight away replicated the original results. We spent the rest of the day extending the search, looking for the boundaries of the sub-surface contacts.

We found that the low walls appear to extend the full length and width of the floodplain field, a kilometre long by half a kilometre wide, in parallel rows every 10 paces or so apart. That explains why the field appears to be as flat and level as a snooker table: the sand-laden winter floods appear to have deposited their load in between these walls over the millennia and, every winter, the floods scour the whole field level.

As a result of our informal search, it was decided to seek permission from the landowner to carry out a more formal survey. As you can imagine, there's a constant stream of people looking to do surveys of various kinds in this area, and it took some time to establish our bona fides. However, we finally received permission to survey a 40 m x 40 m grid with a small team of volunteer diviners from the Society, and the results are shown in the diagram.

The black lines comprise 1 m^2 contacts on a 32 m x 32 m grid, and clearly show a north-south trend. Divining isn't an exact science and anomalies can occur depending on the individual levels of experience, sensitivity and powers of concentration; nevertheless, the result is sufficient to warrant further investigation.

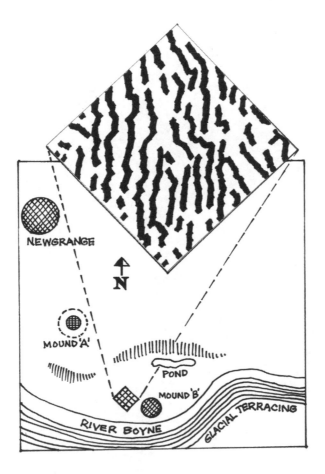

So now will you believe me?

Hugh Kearns
10 Old Ballinalea
Ashford
October 2005

ENDNOTES

1

[1] Michael J. O'Kelly, *Newgrange: Archaelogy, Art and Legend*, London: Thames & Hudson 1982. See Plans & Elevations, Frances Lynch, p. 11 and *passim*.

[2] Martin Brennan, *The Stars and the Stones*, London: Thames & Hudson 1983, *passim* and *The Boyne Valley Vision*, Portlaoise: The Dolmen Press 1980, p. 28.

[3] Martin Brennan, *The Stars and the Stones*, pp. 10–11.

[4] Iain MacDonald (ed.), *Saint Patrick*, Edinburgh: Floris Books 1992, p. 53.

2

[1] P. A. O´Síocháin, *Ireland: A Journey into Lost Time*, Foilsiúcháin Eíreann 1982, p. 75.

[2] Michael J. O'Kelly, *Newgrange: Archaeology, Art and Legend*, London: Thames & Hudson 1982, p. 73.

[3] Ibid., p. 43, where he quotes S. H. O'Grady, *Silva Gadelica*, London 1892, p. 101.

[4] Ibid., p. 43ff.

[5] Ibid., p. 126.

[6] Ibid., p. 123.

3

[1] Claire O'Kelly, *Illustrated Guide to Newgrange*, published by herself, Cork 1971, p. 72, *passim*.

2 Michael J. O'Kelly, *Newgrange: Archaeology, Art and Legend*, London: Thames & Hudson 1982, p. 43.
3 Martin Brennan, *The Stars and the Stones*, London: Thames & Hudson 1983, p. 20ff.
4 Joseph Raftery (ed.), *The Celts*, Dublin: The Mercier Press 1964, for RTÉ, The Thomas Davis Lecture Series; Prof. Kenneth Jackson, *The Celtic Aftermath in the Islands*, p. 75; he quotes Cormac, Bishop of Cashel, *Glossary*, 10th century.
5 George Coffey, *Newgrange and Other Incised Tumuli in Ireland*, Dublin: Hodges, Figgis & Co. Ltd 1912.
6 Michael J. O'Kelly, ibid., p. 36; Richard Burchett, report, Society of Antiquaries of London, 1874.
7 Michael J. O'Kelly, ibid., p. 35, *passim*.
8 George Coffey, ibid., preface.
9 Michael J. O'Kelly, ibid., p. 42.
10 Peter Harbison, *Pre-Christian Ireland from the First Settlers to the Early Celts*, London: Thames & Hudson 1988, p. 63.
11 Michael J. O'Kelly, ibid., *in toto*.
12 Ibid., preface, p. 12, Appendix H, p. 230; Peter Harbison, ibid., p. 10; Sean P. O'Riordáin, *Antiquities of the Irish Countryside*, 5th ed., revised by Ruaidhrí de Valera, London and New York: Methuen & Co. 1984, p. 9.
13 Michael J. O'Kelly, ibid., p. 123.
14 Ibid., p. 92.

4

1 Michael J. O'Kelly, *Newgrange: Archaeology, Art and Legend*, London: Thames & Hudson 1982, p. 110.
2 OPW statistics as of October 2005.
3 Michael J. O'Kelly, ibid., p. 23
4 Ibid., p. 124.

5

1 George Eogan, *Knowth and the Passage Tombs of Ireland*, London: Thames & Hudson, 1986, p. 137.
2 Michael J. O'Kelly, *Newgrange: Archaeology, Art and Legend*, London: Thames & Hudson, Appendix H, p. 230.
3 Ibid., p. 45.
4 Ibid., *passim*.
5 Ibid., p. 122.

6

1 P. A. O´Síocháin, *Ireland: A Journey into Lost Time*, Foilsiúcháin Éireann 1982, p. 70.
2 Stephen W. Hawking, *A Brief History of Time*, New York: Guild Publishing/Bantam Press 1988, p. 13, *passim*.
3 George Coffey, *Newgrange and Other Incised Tumuli in Ireland*, Dublin: Hodges, Figgis & Co. Ltd 1912, pp. 39–40, quotes Wilde, 1849, 'perhaps were used for some anterior purpose'.
4 Michael J. O'Kelly, *Newgrange: Archaeology, Art and Legend*, p. 34; he is dismissive of Pownall and Macalister.
5 Ibid., pp. 148–9.
6 George Coffey, ibid., p. 16.
7 Michael J. O'Kelly, ibid., p. 39.
8 Ibid., p. 124.
9 Martin Brennan, *The Stars and the Stones*, London: Thames & Hudson 1983, p. 80.
10 Michael J. O'Kelly, ibid. (Claire O'Kelly, Part 1, Introduction), p. 13.

7

1 Peter Harbison, *Pre-Christian Ireland from the First Settlers to the Early Celts*, London: Thames & Hudson 1988, p. 77; Michael J. O'Kelly, *Newgrange: Archaeology, Art and Legend*, London: Thames & Hudson 1982, pp. 117–18; he also quotes Professor Frank Mitchell (1976: 130) and Professor Colin Renfrew (1979: 213).
2 Michael J. O'Kelly, ibid., p. 115.
3 Ibid., p. 116.
4 Ibid., p. 40; he is sceptical of R. A. S. Macalister (1935: 65) and is elsewhere (p. 42) dismissive of his 'threepenny guidebook' (1939).
5 George Eogan, *Knowth and the Passage Tombs of Ireland*, London: Thames & Hudson 1986, p. 146.
6 Michael J. O'Kelly, ibid., p. 124; he quotes Dr Jon Patrick (1974: 518–19).

8

1 Michael J. O'Kelly, *Newgrange: Archaeology, Art and Legend*, London: Thames & Hudson 1982, p. 26; he quotes Herity (1967: 130).

[2] Ibid., p. 116 f; he disagrees with Mr R. Clark of the Geological Survey, whose report is quoted by George Coffey, *Newgrange and Other Incised Tumuli in Ireland*, Hodges, Figgis & Co. Ltd 1912, p. 17.

[3] Martin Brennan, *The Stars and the Stones*, London: Thames & Hudson 1983, *passim*.

[4] Attributed to Alec Issigonis, the designer of the 'mini' car, on his dislike of working in teams; *Guardian* '*Notes and Queries*' 14 January 1991, *Oxford Dictionary of Quotations*.

[5] Peter Harbison, *Pre-Christian Ireland from the First Settlers to the Early Celts*, London: Thames & Hudson 1988, p. 76; he quibbles with O'Kelly's architectural analysis, although O'Kelly acknowledges the broken joints (1982: 119).

[6] Michael J. O'Kelly, ibid., p. 124; he quotes Dr Jon Patrick (1974: 518-19).

[7] Ibid., p. 22, p. 119ff.

[8] Ibid., p. 119.

[9] Ibid., p. 120.

[10] Ibid., p. 120.

[11] Ibid., p. 78.

[12] Ibid., pp. 119–20.

[13] Ibid., p. 121.

[14] Ibid., p. 100.

9

[1] Michael J. O'Kelly, *Newgrange: Archaeology, Art and Legend*, London: Thames & Hudson 1982, p. 34.

[2] Caitlín Matthews, *The Celtic Tradition*, 'Elements Of' series, Dorset: Element Books Ltd 1989, p. 83ff.

[3] Michael Herity, *Irish Passage Graves*, Dublin: Irish University Press 1974, p. 136. Photograph attributed to the Director, Irish National Museum.

[4] Claire O'Kelly, *Illustrated Guide to Newgrange*, published by herself, Cork 1971, p. 106.

[5] Michael J. O'Kelly, ibid., p. 96.

[6] Ibid., pp. 35-6; he quotes Wilde (1847), but there appears to be an inconsistency in defining the stones. Could it be that the closing stone was the remarkably carved stone 'which now slopes outwards from the entrance'?

[7] Ibid., p. 98.

[8] Ibid., p. 102.

10

[1] Michael J. O'Kelly, *Newgrange: Archaeology, Art and Legend*, London: Thames & Hudson 1982, pp. 123–4.

[2] Ibid., p. 127.

[3] P. A. O'Síocháin, *Ireland: A Journey into Lost Time*, Foilsiúcháin Eíreann 1982, pp. 15–16.

[4] John Mitchell, *Megalithomania: Artists, Antiquarians and Archaeologists at the Old Stone Monuments*, London: Thames & Hudson 1982, p. 142.

[5] Michael J. O'Kelly, ibid., p. 33.

[6] Ibid., p. 117; he computed the latter total from Professor Frank Mitchell's own figures in *The Irish Landscape* (1976).

[7] Ibid., p. 72.

[8] Ibid., p. 73; he dismisses Macalister again.

[9] Kurt Mendelssohn, *The Riddle of the Pyramids*, London: Thames & Hudson 1974, *passim.*

[10] Michael J. O'Kelly, ibid., p. 33.

11

[1] Michael J. O'Kelly, *Newgrange: Archaeology, Art and Legend*, London: Thames & Hudson 1982, p. 73. He speculates that an earth tremor may have been responsible for a *secondary* slide of material some time after the main collapse.

[2] Michael Herity, *Irish Passage Graves*, Dublin: Irish University Press 1974, p. 200.

BIBLIOGRAPHY

Bord, J. and Bord, C., *Mysterious Britain*, St Albans, Herts.: Paladin 1975.

Boylan, H., *A Valley of Kings: The BOYNE: Five Thousand Years of History*, Dublin: O'Brien Press 1986.

Brennan, M., *The Stars and the Stones*, London: Thames & Hudson 1983.

Burl, A., *Prehistoric Astronomy and Ritual*, Aylesbury, Bucks.: Shire Publications Ltd 1983.

Coffey, G., *Newgrange and Other Incised Tumuli in Ireland*, Dublin: Hodges, Figgis & Co. 1912.

Eogan, G., *Knowth and the Passage Tombs of Ireland*, London: Thames & Hudson 1986.

Fagan, B., *New Treasures of the Past*, London: Grange Books 1992.

Francis, P., *Brú na Bóinne Sí an Bhrú*, Dublin: An Gúm 1991.

Greene, D. H., *An Anthology of Irish Literature*, New York: New York University Press 1954.

Harbison, P., *Pre-Christian Ireland: From the First Settlers to the Early Celts*, London: Thames & Hudson 1988.

Harbison, P., *Guide to National and Historic Monuments of Ireland*, Dublin: Gill & Macmillan 1992.

Hawking, S. W., *A Brief History of Time: From the Big Bang to Black Holes*, London: Guild Publishing 1991.

Herity, M., *Irish Passage Graves*, Dublin: Irish University Press 1974.

Herity, M. and Eogan, G., *Ireland in Prehistory*, London and New York: Routledge 1989.

Kinsella, T., *The Táin*, London and New York: Oxford University Press, in association with Dublin: Dolmen Press 1970.

Kinsella, T., *Butcher's Dozen*, Dublin: Peppercanister 1972.

Mac Cana, P., *Celtic Mythology*, Middlesex: Newnes Books 1985.

MacCulloch, J. A., *The Religion of the Ancient Celts*, London: Constable & Co. 1991.

MacDonald, I. (ed.), *Saint Patrick*, Edinburgh: Floris Books 1992.

MacNeil, E., *Phases of Irish History*, Dublin: M. H. Gill & Son Ltd 1937.

Mallory, J. P. and McNeill, T. E., *The Archaeology of Ulster: From Colonisation to Plantation*, Belfast: Institute of Irish Studies, Queen's University Belfast 1991.

Mendelssohn, K., *The Riddle of the Pyramids*, London: Thames & Hudson 1974.

Michell, J., *Megalithomania: Artists, Antiquarians and Archaeologists at the Old Stone Monuments*, London: Thames & Hudson 1982.

O'Brien, T., *Light Years Ago: A Study of the Cairns of Newgrange and Cairn T Loughcrew Co. Meath Ireland*, Dublin: The Black Cat Press 1992.

O'Kelly, C., *Illustrated Guide to Newgrange*, published by herself, 1971.

O'Kelly, M. J., *Newgrange: Archaeology, Art and Legend*, London: Thames & Hudson 1982.

O'Riordáin, S. P. (ed.), *Antiquities of the Irish Countryside*, 5th ed., revised by Ruaidhrí de Valera, London and New York: Methuen & Co. 1984.

O'Síocháin, P. A., *Ireland: A Journey into Lost Time*, Foilsiúcháin Éireann 1982.

Piggot, S., *British Prehistory*, London: Oxford University Press 1955.

Raftery, J. (ed.), *The Celts*, Dublin: The Mercier Press 1964, for RTÉ, The Thomas Davis Lecture Series.

Rolleston, T. W., *Celtic Myths and Legends*, London: Studio Editions 1986.

Smyth, D., *A Guide to Irish Mythology*, Dublin: Irish Academic Press 1988.

Wentz, W. Y. E., *The Fairy – Faith in Celtic Countries*, Gerrards Cross, Bucks.: Colin Smythe Ltd 1988.

Wernick, R., *The Monument Builders*, Holland: Time-Life Books 1979.

INDEX

ACKNOWLEDGMENTS

Grateful acknowledgment is made to Mr William Redhouse and his son David of Newgrange Farm for permission to carry out the survey on their lands.

Many thanks to the members of the Irish Society of Diviners: Ms Moya Henderson (Hon. Secretary), Ms Catherine Dargue, Ms Mary Reynolds, and Mr Degnán Geraghty, for their dedicated expertise at short notice.

Sincere thanks to Mr Don Brennock for trojan work in laying out the survey grid.

This edition rejoices in an incisive edit by Kristin Jensen, for which we are all grateful.

The first edition and first reprint of this book were printed and published by Pat Funge at the Elo Press. An extraordinary man by any standard, Pat – or Paddy, as he was fondly known by the members of the Lantern Theatre – had more facets to his character than the crown jewels. This poem, read by the poet Francis Devine at Pat's funeral mass, is so sharp a picture of him it's as though Francis had secretly observed our many conversations standing on the print-shop step. Ní bheidh a leithéad arís ann.

Printer and Devil
for Patrick Funge (1929–2001)

At the print-shop step we stand,
chill wind billowing our shirts,
blethering ten-to-the-dozen –
football, politics, art,
memory, personality and tall tale.
I drive away with a job well done,
a smile on the face, a lift in the heart.

Rule and margin, header and footer,
landscape and portrait, foolscap and bond:
I repeat all after him while he eye-glasses the page,
queries the grammar – obscure language always
   winning
over ill-chosen modernity – yet freshness and
   innovation
mark his craft, his gentle handling of text, tone
and illustration: no child leaves his care with hair
   uncombed,
tide-lined neck or an absence of manner.

I wonder as he disputes vellum or board,
while he mutters about Houndstooth, Wing-ding,
Haettenschweiler, Tahoma or Antique Olive,
my Times New Roman seeming sadly commonplace:
his view always from the mountain top,
mine from the valley floor.
Ems and point-size, stencil and disc,
scanning and binding: each become clear
from a laughing, casual tuition,
a trust of judgment drawn on practised method,
certain and rewarding.

At the print-shop step we stand
disagreeing over wrongs and rights,
Thatcher and Spring, a global prospect
through the needle-eye of Dolphin's Barn.
Ready couplets and appropriate gobbets illuminate
the eternal capacity of theatre, the flippancy of
    Hollywood:
Behan's intention, Friel's genius,
Kernoff's cuts and McAnally's diction are grangerised
then closely proofed for flaw and marginal correction.
A deep guffaw ever holds the fall,
softens the blow, floats above the merely don and
    devil,
stains my fingertips magenta and cyan,
yellow and black
and sets the echoing characters
that will certify my place of informal learning,
be read as evidence of a wonderfully valued friendship.